"What sets *Mining Your Past* apart from all the other how-to books out there for writers is Zuras's willingness to put his own work on the line. He doesn't just preach his advice for fiction and poetry; he practices it, and he's willing to show the novice what he's done and why."

—Lucy Ferriss, author of *Foreign Crimes: Stories*

# MINING YOUR PAST

# MINING YOUR PAST

A Creative Writing Professor's Guide
Writing Stories, Poetry, and Song Lyrics

*Richard Lee Zuras*

BELLE ISLE BOOKS
www.belleislebooks.com

ISBN: 978-1-958754-03-0
LCCN: 2022917102

Printed in the United States of America

Published by
Belle Isle Books (an imprint of Brandylane Publishers, Inc.)
5 S. 1st Street
Richmond, Virginia 23219

BELLE ISLE BOOKS
www.belleislebooks.com

belleislebooks.com | brandylanepublishers.com

*I would like to thank my supportive students and every great teacher I ever worked with, especially Robert Olen Butler and John Wood, as well as my colleagues past and present.*

*This book is dedicated to my wife, Kelly, and our sons, Holden and Everett, with love, and with the hope that art always plays an important role in their lives.*

# TABLE OF CONTENTS

## *South of Interstate 10*

*(for John Wood)*

The poet came to our student parties,
The poet in his seersucker suit,
The poet in his mint green pants
Serving his mint green julips.
The poet's grin belied imperfect
Teeth, hair tousled like youth
His laughter infectious. . . .

The poet held the gods of poetry
Within him, reciting lines at will:
St. Vincent Millay, Joyce, Shakespeare,
The poet stirring julips with home-made
Sugar-swizzle sticks. What fun we had.
All from elsewhere, thrust into the poet's world:
Louisiana, land of Zydeco, land of Mardi-Gras

Parades. The poet dancing on the counter,
Drink in hand, legs crossed and kicking
Like a child pleased with his deeds, watching us
Drink his nectar. The poet in his seersucker suit,
Wondering if we understood. Outside looking in,
We wondered if he was teaching us poetry,
The poet, or crafting a cult of poets meant to replace.

# INTRODUCTION

**BY THE END OF THIS BOOK,** you will see I have written to you from a place you rarely see. I have painstakingly exposed my entire process, and everything I teach here can easily be extracted; you simply use the same methods I show you and replace my world with yours. I am not showing you how to write like me; I am showing you from where I write, and how I find my writing and make my writing, so that you can do the same with your own. It is not a trick; it is about learning how to mine your past (and your present) in order to realize your truthful world. Once you do this, writing will always be an option for you to explore your reality. In addition, if you write genre fiction rather than literary, the truths and methods you learn can easily be adapted. In other words, at the heart of science fiction, young adult, horror, etc., lies truths from that author. You will get nothing here but truth.

So: Who am I? I am a creative writing teacher with over twenty-five years of teaching experience at three different universities. I have taught fiction writing and poetry writing to nearly one thousand students, many of whom had never written creatively or had only taken a class unit in high school. I was tenured in 2005 and earned a position as full professor in 2011 at the University of Maine at Presque Isle. I have never lost my zeal for teaching my students to find their creative center. I have published a few dozen stories and poems in literary journals like *Story Quarterly, Laurel Review,* and *South Dakota Review*. I also have published two novels and a book of poems with Brandylane Publishers in my home state of Virginia.

I have held conference-long creative writing scholarships at Bread Loaf and Wesleyan University, and I earned my MA and MFA under Pulitzer

Prize winner in fiction Robert Olen Butler and two-time Iowa Prize winner in poetry John Wood in 1998.

In addition, I have studied and learned under live instruction from: Lucy Ferriss, Lucia Berlin, Alan Cheuse, Jay Meek, James Robison, Carol Anshaw, Ron Carlson, Daniel Wallace, Tony Hoagland, Susan Dodd, William Miller, Dean Young, Chris Offutt, Van Jordan, David Milofsky, Ron Sukenick, and others. I was also fortunate to attend my MFA classes with Pulitzer Prize winner in fiction Adam Johnson and Pulitzer Prize finalist in poetry, Morri Creech. I owe them all a debt of gratitude.

Admittedly, I have no formal training in writing song lyrics, but I have written well over a hundred songs and am the lyricist for my sons' music group, Holden & the Dangers. You can listen to songs I have written for their band here: www.holdenandthedangers.bandcamp.com/releases.

I am also a writer who learned my craft, not a rare-born writer destined for stardom. I was a business major when I began college, though I floundered. I had interest in psychology (and ended up taking many psychology classes) as well as English. All I knew was that I had always enjoyed writing— that I liked creating with the written word. And I knew I had honesty and access to a wealth of memories that would continue to fill in as I aged. My process was developed over the last thirty years from the moment I became a creative writing student at George Mason University in the late 1980s. It is a process that can work for any writer. It can work for you.

*Note: You should only dig deeply into your life, mine your past, if you feel comfortable doing so. If you do not, you can still use this book by applying your own brake when you reach something uncomfortable. No matter what,* you *are in charge of what* you *discover, how you use it, and where* you *apply the brakes. Even as we live our lives, we are making a fiction of it, and so too will you do so by using this book.*

# FICTION

# —1—

# Your Characters Already Exist

## *Breaking rules and a note on tense and point of view*

I have not included many exercises in this book. Too many books over-rely on that strategy rather than actually providing a way for anyone to access the writing within them. This one exercise, however, is crucial in that it allows you, immediately, to find and create real characters. It is something you will use from now on.

Simply make a list of everyone you have ever known, or currently know, or even people you only kind of know. Include family or do not. You decide who goes on the list. This list can also serve your poetry writing.

When you have written down all the names, you can now make a new file wherein you write down things that are interesting about them, good and bad. Write down how you think they see the world. Write down events and stories you remember. Be brief but get down enough to spark the memory again.

After you have a bunch of these done, throw away the actual name list: delete all attached names.

Take a day or a week away from the list.

Then take some of these trait lists and work with them, crossing out some things and adding others until they no longer truly match the original person. You might try blending some of these people together, where three people become two people, or two one. Sometimes this naturally happens, this deleting and adding and blending, as you write the fictional work. That is encouraged. Try to stay true to the original idea of this person, but feel free to embellish and take educated guesses about their world. Keep going until the person feels like a new acquaintance

Now you have a working list of characters.

Another way to do this "finding of characters" is to use people from your life, but place them in situations they have not been in. Then, exaggerate their truths for drama or comedy and let them exist as characters, not actual people, as they come to life.

An example from my own work is the story I published entitled "So Mother Left Father." In this story I used my parents as base characters. My parents were never divorced, but I wondered how that would go, especially if they divorced at middle-age. As the story took shape it was easy to see that these characters, once exaggerated, found themselves in a comic story.

These characters, as I wrote, exaggerated, and manipulated events, became characters informed by and inspired by my parents, but they were no longer real people. That does not mean my characters do not bear some resemblance to real people at times, and thus you must know that it is your decision whether to do this and, if so, to what degree. Even if you completely get away from real friends and family members, they will still see themselves in these characters if and when they read your work. What you write is your responsibility, and if you work from reality, you must accept the consequences, as people will be happy—or not happy— with what they see in your work as it relates, correctly or incorrectly, to them. In other words, if you write a character that is the "mother" in a story, your mother will naturally assume the character is her.

It is also important for you to know whether or not you are mentally and emotionally okay to write from a place of truth. That is your personal decision and one that should be made, consistently, with an understanding that truth has a price. Honesty affects the writer and the reader. But make no mistake: most writers are using *some* honesty in their work. My aim is to be upfront about what this means and how you can most easily find and work with honesty. I began writing from truth when I was in my twenties, but everyone gains the perspective to work with their heavier emotions at different points in life and for myriad reasons. And, of course, the more realism a story contains, the more truth it requires. I am a realist. In "So Mother Left Father" I tried to also play the narrator to comic levels, and obviously some of the narrator was based on me. This is an important element of writing. If you write from a place of truth, be sure that whichever character is informed from your life is also treated honestly, and yet be sure also that the character is manipulated. I liken this to looking at multiple photos of someone when they are both very young and very old (often done on an app these days). In the photo at an older age, you can still see that youthful person in the young photo. However, additions and subtractions have been made; the person has been manipulated by the forces of time, the forces of aging, the forces of life.

In this story, which I wrote and published in a top literary journal, I strived to achieve such an honesty even within the humor: that honesty came from basing the characters on real people. I read this story at a bookstore to kick off my university's reading series. After the reading a young man came up to me and told me that he commiserated and that the story made him understand, or at least contemplate differently, his parents' divorce. He said something I don't recall but it brought forth my admission that my parents had never divorced. The young man was perplexed by this. Though I did not intend to deceive him personally, my job as a fiction writer—one who is steeped in writing from truth—was marked a success.

Here is the beginning of the story:

## *So Mother Left Father*

When your mother left your father, you probably weren't around to see it. You were at soccer practice, or at a friend's house chewing the hard, pink sticks of gum that came pressed between the likenesses of Carlton Fisk, Jim Palmer, and Catfish Hunter. Maybe, if it happened early enough in your lucky little life, you still remember those baseball cards—the batting averages, the earned run averages, whether they batted left but threw right—better than you do *your father*. Or maybe you do remember him, maybe you saw him on alternate weekends, alternate holidays, alternate graduations. Maybe you remember him but have no likeness of them. Maybe you had a baseball mitt at each house, separate baseball caps, separate batting stances. Maybe for one you threw left; for the other you threw right.

You were probably young enough, in any case, to reap the rewards of divorced parents. You learned how to cast them against one another. *But Dad always lets me watch wrestling. But Mom always lets me choose the restaurant. Why can't you be more like him? Like her? Like him? Like her?*

You are also able, now, to blame everything on their divorce. *Of course I'm in therapy! My parents divorced when I was just a child. A child! Imagine the damage!*

You were lucky. You have *no* idea what divorce is.

My parents divorced last year.

I'm thirty-three years old.

•••••

It wasn't a typical day at all. For one thing, my mother's Buick was parked diagonally on their lawn. At first I thought she was acting like all the suburban clowns we live near—pulling up to the stoop to wash the family car in range of the television, listening to Oprah or Springer and laughing about the problems those *other* people have in their humdrum little lives. I was coming home from softball practice, from the *International Business Computers Systems Redhens* team, which I managed, awkward bat bags slung over my shoulder for the short walk up to their house, for a "dinner visit" as my mom liked to call it. Her Buick, I noticed, had an indent just left of center making a kind of "V" in the grille.

Inside everything seemed normal (although everyone always says "that was normal for *our* family"). My father was busy not watching television, which for him meant the volume was on high and he was occupying the closest possible seat to the set, a Blatz to his right (or a Red White & Blue, or a Pabst Blue Ribbon, or Old Milwaukee, whatever was the bare bottom cheapest—if you're going to rot your gut, my father used to say in defiance of my gaze, "use rot-gut"), a television directory spread wide open across his lap (as if something else might be on to *not* watch), and a box of snotty, wadded Kleenex to his left, like a living, micro-biotic border between himself and whoever might consider trying to share his couch.

I said, "Hey" and he grunted, a kind of convulsive shoulder move I had come to interpret as "I'm same as usual and your mom's in the kitchen why don't you go bug her and leave me be can't you see I've had a hard day?" Thing is, it was Saturday, and we all had the day off. I wonder now if that isn't the deep-rooted problem with all of us. By Wednesday everyone in your office starts harassing you with that nonsense. *So, what are you going to do on your days off?* I know guys who work every day of the week just to avoid days off. It's daunting. You not only have to spend the last half of the week promoting your upcoming days-off choices, you have to spend the first half of the week defending your previous choices.

Next weekend, you say, will be different. Better.

Then, next weekend comes and you find yourself in the kitchen with your mom and she's got all her Tupperware out, even the disposable ones, and a fat black permanent pen in one hand and a roll of masking tape in the other. And, like I did, you say, "Mom, what *are* you doing?"

Mom looked at me without looking at me, the way my mom and your mom and her mom learned to do, a skill they perfected when we were young (we were all young once they say and you try to *fathom* such an idea), and she said just four words like she had seen a movie and spent days contemplating another way to say it, all the while unconsciously rehearsing that damned movie cliché, and then she fell back on it in the heat of the moment, as if she had rehearsed the words her whole *life*: I'm leaving your father.

Perhaps you just stare and offer a feeble "what?" Or, like me, you say in diametric opposition to the proud, framed degrees hanging on your office walls something like, "Does he know? I mean, he's in the next room!"

That's what I said. How could he know? How could he just be inert on a Montgomery Ward sofa if she had already told him? She said, "Of course he knows."

Of course. *Of course*. What the hell was I thinking? Is dinner ready? Does Dad need a new beer? Can I get you one Mom? Or have you been drinking since sunup? And what is with all the Tupperware!

"What's with the Tupperware?"

"Been putting up some meals for your father."

"Huh?" Huh? "Huh?"

"You know he doesn't like to cook much, hon. Except for barbecuing. But it's getting nippy to be out there minding that pit. No protection back there, and you know how the wind comes up off that open field."

I'm still stuck on *huh*.

She goes on. "You still want to eat? You hungry? Of course you are. Why don't you set down those things?"

Got to be a joke. Dad and the April fool's jokes. Pretty elaborate with the Tupperware and all. My second year of grad school my dad calls me and says, "Hey, quick, call your mom and tell her you got kicked out." I say, "For what? Cheating?" He says, "Yeah, go with that." And I do. I ring right back and my mom answers and I tell her "Look Mom, I got a bit of bad luck here. I looked at my notes during an exam and I'm up for review board. If they decide to, they can fail me out of here. They've already pulled me off my lab instruction job."

The phone went *dead*.

My mom's heart was breaking. A wound opened up in her. In her voice. In the cracks I heard deep within it. Neither of us said it, but we were both of us flashing to every time I ever cheated. Skipping a turn at Monopoly, moving a chess piece to an incorrect position, faking a fever with a thermometer and one of her plastic Bics. The time two multipacks of gum fell out of my socks in the grocery line.

My dad started losing it in the background. His laugh was at the crossroad of tears.

I wait for it now. My mom writes out *split pea soup* in big block letters, and I drop the bats and wait. Either my dad will laugh or he'll cross right in to tears. Nothing. Not a thing.

•••••

My mom moves into a studio apartment over the newspaper building downtown. She has a half stove. She has half a fridge. I'm surprised the *window* is full. It all seems, I tell her, too real.

"It is real," she says.

It can't be. "It can't be," I say.

"It is," she says. "But it doesn't concern you, hon."

Where parents get these lines is beyond me. My mother doesn't even watch television. She hates movies. She says there's nothing good that can come from watching people that are all better than you. They're all rich, or they can dance, or raise their eyebrows at the right time. Everything, she always said, is too much on cue, and who needs that?

"This isn't on cue at all," I say.

"What?" she says.

"Never mind," I say. But she is right about the movies. No matter what, you are looking up at these giant people on screen the way you look up at the stars in autumn. Science tells us none of these stars are actually there, not as you see them. And what is the point of gazing and longing for something that isn't even real?

My mom's apartment is furnished like a college student's. She has a silver television, used as a plant stand, atop a dark grey milk carton that says *Do Not Steal This Milk Crate,* a very used looking fold-out futon bed with a giant Chinese character in its middle, and an army-navy-sized spaghetti pot. That's about it save for the closets.

"What are you doing, Mom? What are you doing here?"

•••••

My father is sitting on the couch. It's been a month of Saturdays already. We're not watching *Hogan's Heroes* together on TV Land. I've come to mark our time through a watchful eye of Dad's dead soldiers. When he flattens the fourth beer can in the wall-mounted can crusher at the entrance to the kitchen, I know to rise and announce my departure. My father, it seems, has taken early retirement. He tells me this as I step out into the night's chilly, welcome air. It was the day before my mom, he says before closing the door behind me, "made all those Tupperware meals."

"Mom, I know why you left," I say as I enter her apartment. "We can fix this. It's just nervousness. A step. A stage. That's all."

"Honey," she says, "you haven't even entered stage one yet. Talk to me when you're in my shoes."

Has she always talked to me this way? You live under my

roof; you live under my rules. Because I said so, that's why. Life isn't always fair. Would you like it if I did that to you? You'll understand one day. Yes, I think, she has always talked to me this way.

"You're fifty-four years old, Mom."

"Fifty-five, hon."

"Exactly," I say. Then I check the math in my head for a moment. "Exactly," I continue. "You can't get a divorce, Mom. I don't think it's even legal for you to divorce Dad," I say.

She gives me the you-really-are-still-five-years-old glare and I hit her with "Mom, you're acting like a child." I'm flailing my arms around a bit as I say this.

"Hon," she says, "stop flailing your arms around. Have you always been like this?" she says.

Back to Dad's house. I say, "Dad, you've got to go back to work. You're scaring Mom with the threat of your retirement." Retirement, I think, is a life-long sentence of weekends. A life-long sentence of planning and justifying, justifying and planning. It already scares the crap out of me. Hell, I don't even like softball, and I've been coaching Saturdays for eight years.

"I am retired," he says. "I'm not going to un-retire."

"Dad, you're still young," I say. "You've got so much ahead of you. You've got so much time."

"What time is it?" he says. He holds up his retirement watch to his ear. "Forgot to wind it," he says.

At work I keep making excuses on Wednesdays as to why I can't coach on Saturdays. On Mondays I try to remember the excuse I gave. Eventually I tell them my parents are sick. Every Wednesday they say *both of them*? and I say *yes, both of them.*

---

Humor is actually more difficult to write than drama, at least for me and also, I believe, for most of my students. The best humor comes from an honest place. This is where mining your past and exaggerating personal foibles of real people keeps the humor grounded. When I was young, I wanted to be a stand-up comedian. The comedians I most respected were the ones who did not tell jokes but told stories from their lives that were based in truth, even when hyperbole found the laugh. Funny thing is, I joke around in life but rarely write humorous stories. Truth likely plays a role. My father always used to sit in his living room chair and rip out the ads in *TV Guide Magazine*. That stuck with me, and so in it went. It is that simple. (By the way, I caught myself ripping those ads out years later, probably with the exact face and force my father did.)

When you begin a story, you must have already decided, or soon will need to decide, the tense and the point of view. I wrote "So Mother Left Father" in past tense, then slipped into present tense. To do this on purpose is an advanced move, but if you double back and reread, you will see it did not take much work to do so.

Many of my students slip back and forth between the two tenses, almost always unaware they are even doing so. Choices such as tense and first versus third-person narration need to be purposeful decisions. In addition, they need to be contemplative decisions. The default for most fiction is past tense. Only when you truly believe the story needs to be told in present tense should you do so. I rarely choose present tense, as I feel it is antithetical to the way we naturally tell and receive stories.

Why did I choose present tense here? I believed the humor benefited from the use of present, and more so, I felt it worked well to start in past and move to present tense, as the story begins in macro, outside the narrator, and then comes into sharp focus with the present tense inside the narrator's voice and world.

This brings us to perspective. "So Mother Left Father" is ultimately the narrator's story, the way *The Great Gatsby* is ultimately Nick Carraway's story and not Jay Gatsby's. The change in worldview comes to Carraway, not Gatsby. Likewise, in my story, it is the narrator, Lawrence, who may come to see the world differently in the end. And it is that simple, to a point. If a character really owns a story, it is natural to use first person. However, you should have an idea as to whether or not your character will be everywhere you want to be as a writer. If not, it can be easier to choose third person, as the third-person narrator can be everywhere. Second person ("you") is odd and off-putting but can be effective in certain stories. In my story, I actually use it in the first few paragraphs before switching back to the "I" narrator. If something works, it works. Don't be precious about creating art.

So, I effectively switched point of view and tense over the course of telling this story. Notice, though, that the story did not push "experimental" forms and rather played with simple techniques to best tell the story at hand.

Another example of such adhesion to and yet subtle non-compliance with formal rules of writing can be found in another story of mine, entitled "Outside Beach." In this story, I very much assumed my narrator was the one whose worldview would change given the events of the narrative. This is why it can be helpful to think the core of the story through somewhat before writing. I find that I can do just that by walking my dog. I don't take notes, I don't record anything, and yet I envision the story. I refuse to think through the ending. That way when I sit down to write, I am not locked down.

So, I knew my narrator was central; his worldview would change, and so I wanted to use first person. (And, in full disclosure, I do believe that mining one's past more naturally lends itself to the first-person narrative choice.) The trouble was, I knew my narrator would not be present for many of the story's actions. Most writers would then decide on third person. Instead, I elected to write the story in first person. You can read it here and then I will explain how this story was rejected, then eventually accepted, by a respectable literary journal, *and* why my choices angered several literary editors.

## *Outside Beach*

This is the last story I heard about my father.

His name was Jack Grady, and he worked as a rail yard guard north of Denver for twenty-two years before moving my mom and me and our dog Kirkie to a little town called Beach, along the North Dakota—Montana border. I was eleven or twelve at the time and I guess he was near fifty or fifty-one. I was a mistake, my mom's younger sister told me years later. She also told me my father had never wanted kids, had even threatened to give me away a couple years earlier to a Sioux couple he came to know working construction north of Pine Ridge, South Dakota, where the White River snakes its way out of Badlands National Park. But he never did; though I did meet that Indian couple once, by chance, fishing Lake Oahe, ice fishing, where we pulled what I guessed were dead pike out of a frying-pan-sized hole my father had cut out with his hand axe. My father always carried a hand axe with him, even when he wasn't clearing paths through the Badlands National Park, where he worked, or the Teddy Roosevelt National Park, where he also worked. It was a thick handled thing, made of pure ashplant, heavier than it looked, with my father's initials burned into the base of it. But this time I want to tell of had nothing to do with my father's work in the national parks, though it did have something to do with nature. My father had taken to drinking again, especially weekends, something he had not done since we left Denver. My aunt told me years later that he had "jumped right off the wagon." It was the first I had ever heard that he'd had a real drinking problem. Whenever I'd asked my mother, she just shrugged it off and told me "everyone drinks" or that it was just a lot of "bad talk." But this last story anyone knows about my father, he's drunk no matter who tells it. And no matter who tells it, no matter how this detail or that changes, the story always ends up in the same place.

It was the first full winter we had spent in Beach, North Dakota. A couple of weeks into the new year and my father without any steady work. We were living in a trailer, a single wide maybe fifteen by forty feet, the four of us including my mom's sister, who was visiting, and our mutt Kirkie. My mother had taken a job waitressing at a little diner in town, maybe a ten-minute car ride from the farm where our trailer was parked. My father, I remember, joked that we were too far from downtown Beach to hear the ocean. He'd always take me outside to look at the stars when mom would work overnight shifts. And he took me outside the last night I ever saw him.

I could smell the Ben-Gay he always rubbed into his arms, even on days he didn't work. It was a menthol smell, and it's with me so much to this day I can't smell a lit menthol cigarette or walk into a locker room without thinking of him. That night the air seemed very still, and his scent seemed especially strong.

"Good star night," he said. Every night he took me out he said it. He said it if the sky was clear and a whole moon sat up in the dead middle of the sky. He said it if a black snow cloud was sagging low overhead. He said it even on nights when all we could see was the glow of our black and white TV flickering through the trailer windows.

"Great night, Pop." And it was. The steady snow had stopped around supper, and though a new storm was supposed to be arcing its way down, an Alberta clipper, it held off long enough for the moon and the stars to come out again.

"Bother you, son? Your mom working and all?"

"I don't know." I knew though. "I guess," I said.

"Me too," he said. He held an unlit cigarette in his mouth. One of mom's. Every once in a while, he'd strike a chimney match along the edge of his steel-toed boots. Every once in a while, he'd get one to light, and he'd bring it up to the tip of his cigarette and then curse it out with a big blow of his breath.

"Over there, see," he said. He was pointing more with his chin than his hands, which he kept tucked up under his arms. In the distance I could just make out a yellow flare of lights. They looked like one big blur, like when you're at a stop light and it goes yellow and you squint at it and the light of the traffic signal merges with the streetlights and every light blends together and runs soft, incandescent, warm. But the light I was seeing were the lights coming out of downtown Beach.

"One of those lights. Your mother's inside one of those lights." Looking back, it was the first he'd ever mentioned mom when she wasn't around. It's funny how two people can get so intertwined, can become such a pair of one, and then when separated, the one never mentions the other. I've seen the same behavior a dozen times with a dozen couples since. And so I'm always struck by the way a dog will search the entire house, exhaust every room, the moment it knows someone is missing.

"I'm tired," I said. I was always ready to go to sleep just when he'd bring me out to look at the lights. And every night, after I'd look around and notice the same truths—that we were on some guy's farm in a trailer big enough for one, that our car looked like it'd been in a demolition derby, and last, that the accumulation of the winter's snow was not going *anywhere*—I'd tell him I had school the next morning or hockey practice and he'd say "yep" and we'd both of us head back in, brush our teeth, and sack out for the night.

My father didn't move. He didn't seem to be hearing me. His head was cocked away from his body and turned in a profile, and he just sort of leaned toward the lights of downtown Beach.

"You want to go see your mom?"

"Not really," I said. What I wanted to do was to go back inside and crawl under my covers and sleep. It seemed colder the clearer the night sky got. In the moonlight I noticed my father had shaved his face. Usually he wore a short beard all the way down his neck. But in that sparse light I could see patches of red, and the crust of blood where the blade had cut him near his Adam's apple.

"We could go see her," he said. There was a flash off his boot and then it came up and flared again at the end of his cigarette. It was the first time I'd ever seen him smoke a cigarette. He'd play poker sometimes in the summer, out on the red picnic table we always dragged around with us, and sometimes he'd smoke a cigar, if anyone had gotten a hold of a Cuban. "We could you and I, son, get in that pickup truck and we could get on sixteen and drive on into downtown Beach. We could get a scoop of ice cream at your mom's diner. You still like mint chocolate chip? We could get a double scoop sugar cone of mint chocolate chip, each of us, and we could walk on out of there without paying. Without so much as a word to anyone. And we could get back in our truck and take the service road to the interstate and head west. Then we'd be in Montana, just like that." He snapped his fingers as he finished, and then he turned to look at me. His eyes were a little red, I guess from the cigarette smoke, and then he turned and stared back again at Beach.

I said, "I'm too cold for ice cream." But I don't think he heard me.

"We could keep on heading west too, son. We could take turns at the wheel. In Montana, you'd be old enough that nobody would pull you over. Take her easy though. Take it real nice and easy. Just spell me while I took a drink you know? Then before sun-up we'd make Missoula. We could stop in Billings and pick up supplies and gas-up. But we'd eat breakfast in Missoula. How about that? Did you know you could wake up and eat easy fried eggs in a whole other world if you want to? Did you know that?"

"I hate fried eggs," I said.

"You could get some damn pancakes then. Or toast and jelly." He put his arm on my shoulder and squeezed it. Hard.

He looked at me and smiled. "I'm saying a man can get somewhere, you know? We could be up in Glacier National Park by the afternoon and do some fishing in Flathead Lake along the way there. You ever been to Canada?"

I looked at Beach when he said it, like maybe I could see what it was he was looking at. My mother had taken me to see relatives one summer when my father had taken a road paving job through the Rocky Mountains, and my father always wondered where all we'd been while he was gone. I hadn't thought about that summer in years.

"No," I said. Though I wasn't quite sure. We had spent some time in the upper peninsula of Michigan. I figured if we had been in Canada it was only in a car driving, and I didn't think that counted.

"We could go up there. The Glacier National Park stretches right up into Alberta."

"I've never been there," I said.

He crushed the cigarette under the toe of his boot. "Me neither," he said.

I went back inside half expecting him to come get me again. But he didn't. He stood outside in the same spot, his head cocked toward Beach. Toward Mom. Through my bedroom window I could see him shifting his weight from one boot to the other. And occasionally he'd pick up a stone and arch his back and heave it in the direction of the lights. Then I fell asleep.

There was a noise, a sharp metal-on-metal kind of noise and then I heard my aunt say "what's that?" Then my father's voice in a low, rumbly tone said, "Go back to bed Gerty." I stood up and I put on my jeans and my hockey shirt and I peered outside. My father was there, but now he was over by the pickup, and Gerty's hands kept reaching for him and he kept backing away from her. Then I saw her hands grab at his and his hands jerked away and then she ran toward the back of our trailer and he took off running after her. I went out the front door and I came around to hide behind the truck, and I could hear Kirkie's bark coming from different rooms in our trailer, my bedroom, then the kitchen. Then my father yelled "The hell you are. The hell you are." I climbed into the back of the pick-up and laid chest-down against the truck-bed. The metal burned cold into my bare cheek and then a beer can clanked into the corner, emptying the rest of itself under the plastic seats at the base of the truck-bed. Then one door slammed shut, the truck moved to that side, then the other slammed, and the truck rocked back again. I looked up enough to see that the rear windows were closed and I sat up and strapped myself into one of the plastic jump seats. My mother wouldn't let us ride in them, but my father said he'd bought a Brat *because* of those seats, and he'd let us ride in them on short trips. I could tell from the quick start that it was my father behind the wheel. He had a way of popping the clutch so fast that the wheels would spin in every gear. I could hear them pretty clearly through the window, and I hunched down a little so they wouldn't see my hair blowing or anything. I figured my father was just going into town to see mom, but when we came off the farm we made a couple of wrong turns, and then we wound up driving a road I hadn't remembered being on. Everything looked pretty much the same outside Beach. Farm property covered in snow, the occasional John Deere covered in snow, abandoned cars covered in snow. Then I saw a sign that said Wilbaux, two miles, and I knew we'd gone across the border into Montana. We were picking up speed and my feet were getting cold, they felt hard, and for a moment I'd wondered if I'd forgotten to put on any shoes. I looked down and realized I'd grabbed a pair of worn-out sneakers, and I was grateful for a moment, until the pain started up again. There was an old, ripped-up blanket underneath my seat, a little wet from the beer, and I wrapped it around my feet. Then I got nervous again, wondering whether my aunt had actually gotten in the truck. I began to think maybe I'd just heard a woman's voice from the AM radio, and I began to think my father actually was going to wake up in a new place. I started trying to calculate how long it would be before he'd stop in Billings for gas, and whether I had enough money to hop a bus back home. I prayed he'd stay off the interstate at least. I decided if he got on the interstate I'd just turn and bang on the little back window. And then the truck stopped fast and I heard my father say, "Fine Gerty." Then I did recognize her voice, but I couldn't quite hear the words she said.

We went back the way we'd come and I could hear the sound of her voice every mile or so. She was talking real soft, and my father wasn't saying a word. Then we found our way back up the hill behind our trailer and when my father shut off the lights, I could see the lights of Beach come into view again. My father cut the engine and we rolled to a stop in some deep snow by a cottonwood. My father called them snow trees because when they blew their cotton it looked like a little winter storm. I thought that maybe he was thinking that right there in the truck, sitting there with my aunt and looking out over the snow. I heard my father's ring against the glass and the sliding of the panels and then the sound of jazz music coming from the radio. The warm smell of cigarette smoke filled the space around me and then just drifted into the night. We sat there through a couple of songs and then the DJ came in and started reading public service announcements and then the radio went dead. The door on my side opened and I could hear my aunt give a little cough and then the door shut again. When my father got out, I looked up over the roof. I could see he had caught up to her and they had started talking again. When I got inside I had to grab Kirkie and muzzle him. He let out a little wincing noise then followed me sleepily into bed. I thought about watching them through the window but before I could even get the covers up and around me I was out cold.

•••••

All of that I know happened. The rest of that night, from three a.m. on, I know only from my aunt. It was years before she told me everything, around the time I turned eighteen and moved up into Manitoba away from her and my mother. She said a *story* is something you hear from a person you don't know. But when someone who loves you tells you things about a loved one, that's called *truth*. My aunt also said you have to accept things as absolutes, hold them like truths, or they will eat at you forever. And I think maybe I believe that absolutely. The thing is, the truth about my father eats at me too.

My Aunt Gerty and my father got back in his truck around four a.m. with a six pack and a bag of saltine crackers. They were on their way into Beach to see my mother. My father drove and Gerty went up and down the radio dial waiting for a response.

"Right there," my father said. "Go back."

Gerty went left and eased in a country song.

"That'll do," he said. "Tonight, that will just sit up and do."

"Listen Jack. We could just go get breakfast at the truck stop. My treat."

"We're going to the diner, Gerty."

Gerty popped the tabs on two beers and handed him one. "Go easy," she said.

"Always," he said. "What's that they say? Calm, cool and collective."

"I think it's collected, Jack. Calm, cool and collected."

"Oh, right," he said. He turned the volume knob down a bit. "That's one dumb song," he said.

"You picked it, friend."

"I'm your friend, am I?" he said.

"Jack. Look. Of course. I'm just trying to work this through for you. People hit patches, right? Like you hit some ice or something, what's that, you can't see the ice?"

"Black ice," he said.

"Right," she said. She rolled her window down a bit and squinted through the crack. "You hit some black ice and things get a little extreme and then you get a grip again and you just keep going."

"I've hit black ice," he said.

"Yes. Well, not you. My stupid sister has. But she'll come through it eventually."

"That's not what you told me a couple hours ago, Gerty."

Then she was silent for a minute or two. She took his hand when he reached across for another beer and it felt so cold and hard in hers. He left it there and for a moment the ride felt smoother, and then he took it back and slapped it hard and flat on the dashboard.

He said, "That damn old man's touching my wife. You know, Gerty? He's *touching* her." His face seemed to grow larger as he spoke and the pitch of his voice went up and down in waves. It seemed to Gerty like it was cracking, like it must have when he was thirteen or so. She wondered what his face looked like then. Then she said, "What will you do?"

"He's my son, Gerty. How the hell does she think she's going to get him. That's a laugh. You know what that is? That's a damn laugh."

"Look Jack. Be smart about this. That's all I'm saying. Don't make them do things you'll regret."

"I'll regret? I'll regret what they do?" Then he turned and stared at her and for a moment Gerty thought they might go right off the road. Miss a turn altogether and plow right into a snow drift. He looked that wild right then. Like he was capable of doing something. When she spoke again he turned back to the road.

"Jack all I'm saying is this guy's not just a lawyer in Beach. He's also a travelling judge. Circuit court or something. He knows everyone in Beach."

"He don't know me," he said.

She started to say "everyone that matters" but caught herself. Instead she said, "They're all a bunch of crooks."

"Then you tell me how she'll get custody? She leaves me for some old fart judge and she gets custody? A man gets fired twice and he's a drunk? I never hit nobody."

"I know," she said.

"I work you know. I still work."

"I know," she said. "It's just how it is now. Maybe if you don't say anything it'll pass. You know? Maybe you guys just need a cooling off period or something."

"Or something," he said.

From where they parked they could see my mother through the front glass. She was serving pie to a younger lady and at the end of the counter sat a man in a checked homburg reading a newspaper.

"That him?" he said.

"Might be," she said. "I think so. I just know he's in town right now."

Then the both of them watched my mother come up behind the man and place her bare left hand, fingers spread, across his upper back. His face turned in towards her and then she leaned in and kissed him on the mouth. It wasn't a deep kiss, or even a public kiss, but the kind of kiss you see two people give one another when there is something unspoken between them. And then they sat in silence, unable to figure out what to do next. Like they had too many options to choose from, or too few, like they knew any move could be the wrong move, or simply the next one. And then my father told my aunt to get out and she did.

She stood there in the cold, still holding the remaining four beers by their plastic holder, the cans dangling limp at her side. She looked in at my mother who had her back to them, moving a rag back and forth across the counter where the pies and coffee cups and saucers were stacked up. Then she looked back at my father, who was still sitting there, his knuckles all lined up in a row atop the steering wheel. It seemed to Gerty that they, the four of them, did this for some time. The four of them there, all hopelessly intertwined and familiar and so close and just so unaware of each other. Then my father started the car, backed up, and drove away with his lights shut off. It was a moment, Gerty said, that felt less like regret and more like calm. She said it was the only time in her life when she actually heard absolute silence.

After a minute or so the car came back around to the front of the diner. Gerty climbed back in and the two of them headed for the interstate. They got on ninety-four and headed east. They passed Home on the Range and the Chateau de Mores historical site and were coming up on Fryburg before Gerty dared to say a word.

"You miss working here?" she said.

"What, the park? Sure. Teddy Roosevelt was a great man," he said. He grabbed a beer from Gerty's lap, popped the top, and took a long, slow draught. "Warm as hell."

"Maybe," Gerty said, "I should dangle them out the window." Then she laughed. She looked over and tried to read his face by the light of the dash. He took another swallow.

"Let me know when you see the signs for eighty-five south, will you?"

"Sure," she said. She thought to ask him where they were going, but when she looked back at the road she could see the sun coming up straight ahead.

"We're heading straight into that big orange fireball," she said. She was relieved to see it. "We could be in Bismarck in two hours."

The car slowed and he eased into the exit lane and in a moment the sun was no longer in front of them. She sensed where it was, like a plant or a dog might, and turned to her left, and found herself staring at my father, this man she had known for so many years, and with the sun shining from behind his head, in the silhouette, she noticed traces of salt on his cheek bone.

Out her window she watched the southern end of the park roll by. The snow had covered everything in a fresh white down. The trees in the distance looked like giant Christmas trees, and she cracked open her window hoping to gleam the scent of a fresh pine or spruce or fir. By the time they rolled up and across the edges of White Butte she had drifted off into a deep sleep.

•••••

"Up Gerty. We're here. Wake up," he said.

It took her a moment to get herself oriented, and another before she could speak. Then she said, "Where the hell are we, Jack?"

"West of Castle Rock," he said. Then he got out of the car and walked off. She looked around the car for her gloves and found them on the floor in front of her under the beer cans, all empties. It took her a minute or two to catch up to him; his gait was long, and she still felt achy with sleep. She looked back and noticed the car was parked in a kind of makeshift lot with picnic tables sitting here and there, a children's plastic play area, and some swings like you put infants in. No one else had parked there, but there were enough spaces cut out that it had to be more than just a roadside pull-off. When she caught up to him he was sitting on a log and sipping one of their warm beers.

"Don't worry," he said. "I didn't drink while you were sleeping."

"Oh," she said. Then she said, "Thanks."

"We've been here about forty-five minutes or so, maybe less."

"That the last beer then?"

"Yep. Sorry," he said. Then he swallowed the last of it and tossed the empty behind him. "Don't litter," he said. "Keep your National Parks clean and serene."

"Are we in a National Park?"

"No," he said. Then he stood up and opened his arms wide. "We're at the epicenter of the whole damned country." Then he made a turn with his arms still out at his sides. Before he could turn a full revolution, his feet came off the edges of the log and he stumbled back a few feet onto his back. She started toward him but he was back up before she could get to him.

"From here," he said, "we can get *anywhere*."

"I don't get it," she said. She looked around and tried to figure out where they were. "Are we in Wyoming or something?"

"No," he said. "Wyoming. We're in South Dakota sister."

"I'm not your sister," she said.

"Right," he said.

"I think there's a storm coming," she said.

"I think you're right," he said. Then he climbed back onto the log and took out his hand axe. He tossed it at the log and it struck in with its blade. He did this a couple of times. Then he said, "From here a man could wake up anywhere he wanted the next day. In twenty-four hours I could drive my truck almost anywhere from *right here*." He pointed at the ground as he said it, and then he split the log again with his axe.

Gerty sat down and pulled her arms tight around her. Even with the heat the sun had offered the air was still chilly, and the beginnings of snowflakes were edging their way down from above. She could hear the snow give beneath her as she sat, and the crunching noise it gave seemed so familiar, so calm. Then she pulled her hat down over the folds of her ears and just breathed. In the distance she saw Jack toss his axe up and then clap when the axe would give itself over to the weight of its blade and strike itself clean into the log. Then he'd pull it out and toss it upward again. The midday sun was giving in to the roll of the snow clouds and the failing light did its best to gleam the metal of the whirling axe blade.

After a while he stood up on the log and began to toss the axe and then catch it by its short wooden handle. His motion was fluid, jerking his hand in only at the last second, out in front of his chest and a little to his side.

"You're pretty good," she said. "You don't even look scared."

He smiled at this, at this little thing she'd said to him. Then he tossed the axe a little higher, adding one more swing, one more time around, handle over blade, handle over blade. And he never missed. Gerty tried to count the revolutions the way her sister and she had counted the revolutions on their baton. Maybe it was more than twenty, she thought. She watched it come down and she could see his arm rise up from the side, rise up to snatch it peacefully out of the air, then she saw the other come up as well, and neither arm stopped, they reached out to each side and she thought he might turn himself, add one more revolution, and then his right arm did lurch forward, and then she could hear a sound, muffled, and then his eyes grew big and an elbow appeared in front of him, awkward, and then his body gave a little bend forward and then a longer bend backward and the little axe seemed to be pushing at him, pushing at his chest and at his throat. The silence returned to her. The God-awful full-throated sound of complete and utter nothingness.

•••••

I spent the next few years with Gerty and my mother—who were never the same after all of that—in towns like New Salem, Watford City and Lostwood, before we finally settled down just outside Williston, North Dakota. We never talked about any of it, not really, until Gerty told me all this truth, and a week after that I packed up my stuff and headed north into Canada. Once, a few years back, I tried to make my way to the spot where it all happened, down to the geographical heart of America, but I couldn't manage to get past the little town of Buffalo, South Dakota, before heading back. To tell the truth, I doubt I'll ever get all the way there.

But if I do end up there someday, I guess it will be at sun-

> up, and I'll just point myself in one direction or the other and drive out as far as I can get in one lonely day, and then I'll pull off and stop at the first roadside diner I come to, and I'll sit down, very calm, and order a full plate of easy fried eggs and sit there, a man waking up in a new place, and I'll just watch that sun come up again. Maybe then, for me, that will be the end of it. Just maybe.

---

Again, clearly most writers would have chosen to write this story in third person, because the narrator I have chosen is absent from so much of the story. Others would have chosen Gerty, but it is not her story. Perhaps an (overly) experimental choice of narrator would have been the deceased character. This has been done in film and literature. Seems like a trick to me; I like honesty.

I was, ultimately, unwilling to deny the son's point of view. I especially felt it resonated in the final section of the story, though the ending was unknown to me as I wrote. So, rather than goofily stow the narrator away in the back of the truck, I chose to have the story relayed by the narrator as if it were pure fact. After all, were you *this* narrator, you would have no choice but to memorize and internalize *that relayed story* to the point that it became *your story* to tell.

When I submitted this piece to some very good editors at some very good journals, the reaction I often got was incredulity. *How could I do such a thing?* they wrote. One particular editor remarked that the writing was excellent and that he wanted to publish the story, but that he just could not accept the breach of point of view. I did not submit the argument I just wrote in my previous paragraph. I simply kept submitting the story to other journals. Rejection, and learning to handle rejection, is an important part of being an artist.

When the story *was* accepted, I recall the journal's editor remarking that the inventive choice I made is what actually gave him the desire to publish the story. This is a great lesson to learn: believe in choices you make in your writing.

And, again, the father in the story was based on my father but became his own character as I wrote. But the fierce, protective, jealous quality . . . that came from thinking about my father. As did the alcohol. The narrator was based on me, which is to say that some of my real emotions and views of my father were influencing what I wrote and how I wrote it. Only I know what is fact and what is fiction.

When I was in grade school and then middle school, I was the lead actor in all the plays. What that meant for me at the time—and later when I built sets in high school for four years—was that I quickly gained an understanding of how, to be in character, you must believe the words you are saying. So, when writing as a first-person narrator, I need to have some connection with what I write. I may not believe everything, but I must understand, and so I write from my own real-world life and perspective. The narrator is a character, and that character often comes from me; that character already exists. The other characters are born through people in my world, even as they morph away from those origins. Thus, all my characters already exist. I simply fictionalize.

And it is important to note that in third-person point of view, the narrator is in the place of a character, but comes across to the reader as the writer. In first-person point of view, by contrast, the narrator truly is a character. First-person narrators are meant to be the main character.

I have been teaching for over twenty-five years, so I can hear the question now: If the narrator is me, or kind-of me, then isn't the first-person narrator just the writer as well?

Good question, and one my students might ask. The answer is yes and no. The narrator is somewhat you, but so are all the other characters. They are all pieces of you. You created them, even if their origins were people other than you. The narrator is still a character, like the other characters, and is removed from that authorial third-person voice so closely attributed to the author.

I taught screenwriting for many years, as well as academic film courses, which I still teach regularly. That training has led me, along with my early acting days, to think of each character as an actor. Have I written a minor or even major role that a character actor, or at least a new actor, or even a star actor would want to play? Then, I imagine myself playing that role, delivering the dialogue lines, working out the world view. In fact, I am doing this as I write, which means that I am attempting to place myself in that character's position. If you do this, a truth emerges in the character, and thus in the writing. Be filmic as you write. The world has dimensions.

This is not to say that I do not write in third person. That discussion will come.

# —2—

# Your Settings Already Exist

## *Whether many or few*

I chose the town Beach in "Outside Beach" because I wanted its aspirational, non-aspirational name. I had actually lived in a mobile home with my parents when I was in college in Virginia, and had lived in North Dakota for three years, well east of Beach. So, I knew mobile home life, and I knew North Dakota. I did not know Beach, but I based the town on my knowledge of the small towns I had visited throughout my life.

In most stories, I use a real place that I know well for the setting. One such story based on a place I knew well was "1954" written about—and set in— Lake Charles, Louisiana. When my wife and I walked our dog, we would often see the same older couple cruising the neighborhood picking up items from outside neighborhood homes. Many towns, including the one I am in currently, have a system wherein people leave items (that might have been in a yard sale) outside with a "free haul away" sign. One day, this couple—this gentleman—took something from outside our house we had left as free. His truck was old, and quite distinct, and I got a good look at it. It had very little paint. It was free of dents.

A week or so later, while walking our dog, we passed his truck and stopped and took a good look at his yard. Then we walked on.

One day about a month later I was in the library of my university just perusing books. All of a sudden, I found a book that would fill in the final piece of what became "1954." I had been contemplating a story about this man—this older couple—and I had decided on the notion that his collecting had a *purpose* to it. Now, along with a book I had already found on Louisiana flowers, I found a brilliant book on vehicles from the 1950s and sat down. Within a half hour I knew that my story would encompass this man's collecting, his gardens and weeds, and his apparent desire to revisit the year 1954. As I wrote, the rest filled in. Again, I chose a first-person point of view which allowed a truthful glimpse into the world of declining mental health that a third-person point of view would not have allowed. Here is the story:

---

## *1954*

I step into our yard the same as I have every waking morning for some forty years, though today I am amazed at the collection that surrounds me. I must admit now, in my young seventies, I am not always aware of my voice. I know I am speaking, and linking images into words, but I don't know if they're audible. And it isn't because Bonnie is unresponsive. I gaze at the milkweeds that grow up between her feet, knowing that even if she is listening to me, I know she won't understand.

This flux in my yard confuses me. Just yesterday the mailman stood under the hot October sun wringing out the sweaty cloth around his dark neck, looking at my cars, the worn-down machines among the overgrown gardens, and I realized that like any history, my collection is about details.

I can remember any detail from 1954, especially anything to do with the cars. It was the year Bonnie and I married, the year I bought my first car—a Hudson Hornet. I bought it, my father warned me, simply because my name too was Hudson.

But he was wrong about my need, and he would not understand my incessant search to own that car again—to bring back that feeling of completeness that so attaches to youth. As I think of that Hudson I am moving past Bonnie, at my aged speed, with eyes forward. I am dipping in with my shoulder and dangled arm in an effort to touch her the way we touched as dancers. I graze her but am somehow not sensitive to this touch as I plod, eyes straight ahead at the newest addition to my collection. Not that elusive Hudson Hornet, as the wraparound curve of the rear windshield reminds me, but a Hudson Wasp.

I anoint this car as my champion, the nearest I have come to reclaiming my youth, and fluttering my fingers in a triumphant wave I bend slowly with my hands upon my knees and I finger the strip where the black wall and the white wall meet and I am breathing faster now. The smell in my nose is not from this ancient rubber but is somewhat sweeter, lower in my nasal cavity, and my eyes open a little to see the petals of what I realize is a lazy daisy. Pushing down with my hands and up with my knees, I rise from the flowers and lift my head to the sky. The purple clouds to the west are streaked by thin gold arcs in this high Louisiana sky, and I know from the sagging gray clouds below that it is raining again over the Sabine River. The lazy daisy will not open to me nor to the sky until all of these clouds have been spent, and have dissipated eastward toward the lakes. I will check on you later. The petals do not wave or flitter in recognition but it is okay, I know that it is too early for her to open regardless of the clouds' wrath or the sun's position, and glancing at my bare wrist I am struck by my prior obliviousness to time. My movement must now be toward the sundial.

When I turned seventy my bride gave me, as a joke it turned out, a Fossil watch that allowed me to attach a plastic sundial to my wrist. I wore it just once, as we have been obliged to do with such momentary gifts to one another. Now, I find myself anxiously drawn to the working earthenware sundial that occupies the center of our wondrous yard.

I have meant to replace the locks rusted into the chains at the entrance gate. Steadying myself upon the front fenders of this Hudson Wasp, as if Bonnie has spoken, I answer: no, I will not use nor do I require a walker. She knows that, Bonnie does, she knows how fine I get from the door of our plantation home to the flowers and my cars, and back and forth from the sundial. This fender is cool and desert brown between its powdery cancer rots that will barrel through wider each day like honeycombs. This coolness is familiar to me. When I sometimes lose my balance and am out of touch with my cars and Bonnie, it is this deeply feared cold I think of. I un-grip my fingers, sliding one finger gently into the cancer, into the workings of this nestled wasp, and I am somehow steadied again.

This steady feeling is too willing to leave me. It moves around my memory like a man packing in a rush, pulling out every necessary item from the drawers, from under the bed, from beneath the mattress. He is sane enough to find pictures of those he has always loved and recognized. But this steady feeling always leaves.

Steady, Hudson? Bonnie's voice. The same in my memory as now, though there is a hint in her voice that is somehow unsure of me. I am steady, I think, so I answer. But I'm not sure of my voice, so I concentrate everything into my hearing, my most basic function, and I am hearing now only bees and a butterfly's wings striking softly against unopened petals of daisies I have passed, and then with a shuttering noise this moment is gone.

With six-inch steps of my left foot and my right, I am steady and moving, rushing forward, and that Hudson is behind me. I still remember the crash. A sound that you can describe in your mind in its slowest form, in a vacuum where time can't even exist, in images and senses so raw that you can't begin to form the words. Maybe I will find that same model, that Hudson one day, and I will sit again behind its steady wheel.

I have collected these 1954 cars and these words that link their alloys and steel and rods into kick panels and sheets and levers and columns. I know these words and what lives in their bellies, my voice coaxing their names as I stop again, arching and tilting my neck to look between their paths. And from where I am, even now, standing in this spot where I must have that Hudson Hornet, I am listing them as my eyes fall shut.

1954, U.S. models. The Meadowbrook and the Kingsway and the toothy face of the Muntz Jet with its round far-set eyes and windshield split apart like eyebrows. The Powermaster and the Fire Dome and the Kaiser Manhattan, even the Kaiser Henry J at a paltry price of just $1,348 and no cents. But it's not the Hudson Hornet and Bonnie, Bonnie is not waving and hooting from the passenger seat as I drive, nor listening to me tell her stories about the semi-elliptic rear suspension that fuses with me and steadies me as I race.

This smell I am putting syllables to is also behind me, where I cannot find it with my craning neck and throat. Larkspur, Gayfeather, Golden Aster, Fairywand, Candy-root, Bee-balm, Beggar-ticks, Bog Torches. Southern flowers. Louisiana flowers. Our yard.

You don't know these flowers, Bonnie, their patterns and rhythms and webs and stigma, the way the Clematis texensis sticks in the bulb of my throat like sorrow. The way the Willy's CJ-3 clamps its hinged hood in the exact, precise manner that the Dionaea traps its flies.

I can't tell you all this. Sometimes in my vulnerable moments I spit and twist and sputter words like a Packard, like a Studebaker, and I watch you nod in rhythm and smile when you think I've finished my thought. I am not angry, and I am aware that I have reached the sundial now with the last small kick of my steps. I turn, ankle to ankle, toe to toe without glancing at the nose of the sundial's face, and squinting against the sun I see you in the corner of my vision, and I am steadied again. The greens and blues and grays and silvers of my cars sit between us. Noiseless. I must start them someday, one by one, the Nash and the DeSoto and even the blazing Cunningham, 150 miles-per-hour strong.

But I cannot know the workings inside. The combustion, the synapses firing in harmony with each connection, hoses mixing chemicals, creating power and grace. Like that Hudson Hornet. Like you and me. You are so clear to me Bonnie, right now, though I can't see your features. Your image is steady and clear, and I am aware from the rock of my step that I am coming slowly back to you, like rain to river, across this landscape of parts and growth.

---

As first written, "1954" was a *much* longer story. The editor and I pared it down until the story had a rhythm and a purpose, and maintained, in its first-person point of view, an allowance for voice. It is, after all, in first person that we *live* with a narrator, hearing that internal stream of thought, that glimpse into someone else's way of thinking that *no other art form can duplicate.*

It is important to note that setting does not have to be restricted to the exact details of a place, as in "Outside Beach" or "1954."

Setting can also mean the attitude of a place.

Every place I have ever lived has a collective attitude. When I lived in Louisiana, I found many elements of collective attitude, and that collective swirled in my brain. Eventually, I wrote a story about rural wrestling, staged many decades ago, and rather than drawing characters from my life, the characters came from the collective of the setting. The constant interplay between sin and redemption I found in Louisiana took shape as good and evil in a rural wrestling match. In other words, my characters came from a collective rather than from an individual. If you know a place well and have contemplated its idiosyncrasies, most especially its group attitude, you have place as character. You can still use fictionalized characters from your own life as well.

I wrote and then published "The Wrestlers of Evangeline Parish" by working through my insider/outsider interpretation of the collective attitude of Louisiana. Here is an excerpt:

---

Used to be everyone knew of a man named Fritz Fontenot, a German-French fellow who wrestled under the name of "The Father." Wasn't like it is now. No one shaved their head and put on earrings and makeup and all like that. They'd have been run out of town. Fritz and his partner, "Lucifer" used to wrestle out past the outskirts of the city, past Thibodeaux's Fresh Fish, Archambeau's Hardware, and the grocery store run by old man Hebert. They pitched a tent and charged ten cents a head, five for children, and when they were done collecting the gate they went out behind the little portable stage and changed into their outfits. You probably get the picture. The Father and Lucifer would go at it a while, putting each other in countless holds, until The Father would finally pin down old Lucifer for good. But they always made a show of it and all, and the crowd always got their money's worth. But nowadays no one knows why there's no more wrestling out past the city limits. People will tell you it's the booze it brings, or that it stirs up the young folks or like that. But I know the truth. I was there. And if you trust me I'll lay down the truth for you right now. There's a reason there's no more wrestling in Evangeline.

It went like I told you already. The Father and Lucifer always wrestled. It was Saturday nights when it was warm enough, which usually meant every week except for December through February, and of course not around Mardi Gras. They wrestled for I reckon two or three years. Some of the folks in the crowd had been there every week, never missed a match. I'm one of them. No, I ain't going to surprise you at the end with, "I was Lucifer!" or, "I was The Father!" I was too young for it anyway. I was old enough in years to pay a dime but looked young enough that they never asked me for more than a nickel. I'd try to give them both the nickels I brung but they wouldn't take them. So I started finding a kid along the way from my house that wanted to go but couldn't, and I'd bring him along and pay for it. Like I said, I'm an honest man, but sometimes people won't believe you no count anyways.

So I must have seen Lucifer and The Father wrestle more than a hundred times. I swear, it was always different. In the beginning it wasn't much. They'd put each other in those normal wrestling holds like old man Boudreaux had shown us in school. Lucifer'd get The Father's wrist pinned back, his arms up under The Father's chest, and then The Father'd roll over and twist out and put Lucifer in a position looked like a baby in a cradle. Pinned him every time. But they kept varying the holds a little. I swear I don't think they were even rehearsed one bit.

By the time that second spring had rolled around those two had built ropes around their stage and the school had donated mats. Lucifer had started wearing these little horns up in his hair and he'd shaved his beard down into a triangle with one of those curly mustaches. The Father had taken to wearing a loose black robe and a little white collar. He came out to each match with a big, black bible in his hand and he'd give it this great big thump, and he'd toss it into the crowd. Everyone would scramble for it and the people would gather around to see what pages got marked.

---

The same situation applied to my short time living in Virginia Beach. This time, it was the mix of runaway teens and people who lived near the beach but never went to the beach, which I found both understandable and odd: a unique collective attitude. Here is an excerpt from "Runaway":

---

I began to go to the beach to kill time on weekends. For a moment or two, I almost thought I could become one of the runaways you saw down on the strip. I had seen a local newscast not long before where they did a focus piece on the high numbers of runaways in Virginia Beach. One girl, right around my age, answered the news guy by saying, "If you were a runaway in this country, wouldn't you hitch-hike to the beach?" He just smiled, but I don't think he really got her. I did. I remember wanting to go down to the beach and look for her, but it wasn't something I could really do. Like the rest of my friends, we avoided the beach and had rarely ever gone into the ocean. Our parents didn't understand this, but it seemed absolutely reasonable to us.

But with no one around to judge me, I drove down there and just walked around the boardwalk. I felt too much like a phony to hang out with the runaways. What happened was I started going into the arcades—when it rained the runaways always gathered in the arcades—and what I did was I dropped dollar bills behind them. If they didn't see them right away I'd tell them that they must have dropped some money. It was after one skinny, filthy, green-eyed girl thanked me and called me "sir" that I stopped hanging around.

---

In these stories, the towns I had lived in—and surrounding towns I had known or often passed through—provided *both* the characters *and* the setting. So, think about where you have lived or visited, and make a list. Write down the way those towns seem to collectively view the world. The more variance you have in your travels, the more you will recognize the distinctions between these worldviews, and the more you will realize that your characters and settings already exist.

But don't fret if you know only one place. Because if that is the case, then *you know it inside out.* The key, then, is something I often tell my students: realize your reader (writ large) *does not know that place.* They do not know your town, nor its worldview. So, write about the place in depth. You know it inside out.

What you must do, though, and this takes some effort, is see the world you know so well with a fresh and loving, yet *critical,* eye. What small town, for instance, does not have its own traditions? Sure, other small towns might share them, but some don't. Or, think of a big city like New Orleans. Everyone knows what Mardi Gras is, but only someone that lives in New Orleans understands every aspect. Examine what you are seeing as an outsider. Pretend you are studying the event, or tradition, or attitude. Take notes. Question everything as if you were a visitor.

I am often surprised how much students do this without being aware. Then, a topic comes up, something about small-town life, and the stories flow. Even in a class of insiders, eventually someone says something an outsider would, and everyone begins to probe the topic: asking questions, criticizing, laughing, sharing moments of joy and pain.

What is interesting is that when an actual outsider enters the conversation, immediately everyone becomes defensive, usually followed by a laugh and a comment about how the outsider does not understand. Exactly. Have that discussion with yourself in your prewriting stage and take notes or think it through until it imprints on you.

The reader does not understand. You do. You are the only one, in fact, who understands the world the way you understand the world. Now, the task is to write that world. Your characters already exist. Your settings already exist. Now, you just need a storyline.

# — 3 —

# Your Story Lines Already Exist

## *And a note on letting characters make mistakes*

Because you have characters that already exist and because you have settings that already exist, in a way, you already have story lines too. You can practically place your characters within your settings and have a story line automatically. Except you don't quite—not yet. You have a character sketch.

Think of it this way: You are talking to a friend or relative and you say, "Hey, I have a story to tell you." Your listener can't help but listen. Why? Because you said the word "story."

When you are writing a short story, you are telling a story. It is that simple.

A story is a story because it goes somewhere. It says something. A story is a story because it evolves. Because it entertains. And most people want to learn something as well. Generally, if your story entertains me and makes me learn or contemplate something, I am in. And, because I am human, I also want what I contemplate or learn to be about the human condition.

People like to ask where stories come from, and the answer is quite simple: the events in your life. I often tell my students it is not a matter of nothing to write but rather too many options to write about. In a given week, and certainly a given month, many good and many bad things happen in your life. In addition, you have a storage of events in your memory. Most of the time, it is easier to pick from memory. Why? Well, for starters, sheer volume. In addition, memory has already blended and connected for you. Last, if you do this right, you pick something you are emotionally capable of writing. You pick something where the characters are or can be blurred and manipulated to not be, exactly, the real people they are based on. The story and characters are malleable.

An example is in my published story entitled "Your Father and Mine," which came from my real life. The genesis of the story is that when I was living away from my parents in another part of Virginia, a man followed my mother home from her place of work. I can't remember if my mother figured this out first, or if my real-life CIA-analyst father spied the man. Either way, my mother told me this story over the phone. I believe it may have happened more than once. My memory is fuzzy.

Sometime later, I imagined how that might have gone if my father had confronted the man. Then, I sat down to write. I did not want to contemplate the workings of my father's mind and instead wanted his actions to carry the story. I contemplated third person but once again knew that my readers would gain something inherent from a son's perspective on watching his father. And why not? So much of our behavior is influenced by watching our families and friends and caretakers, interpreting and imitating—or countering—their behaviors as we mature. Usually, we do all of this at once.

As I began to write, the line that became the title formed in my mind. Growing up in Arlington, Virginia, in the 1970s and 1980s, this was the question everyone, including school friends, asked one another:

*What does your father do?*

As I wrote, I contemplated this both ways. What does my father do for a living (spy, which was greeted with less reaction than you might think given the geographical area), and what does my father do when stressful things arise?

As the writing progressed, the father character took on traits that both contained my own difficulties growing up in a CIA household, and in addition, worked to *progress* the story at hand. When people say *the story is what matters*, this is what they mean. Everything must bend toward the story.

How many times have I heard a student say that they wrote a scene as they did because that is how events they're drawing from actually happened? *It does not matter*. This is fiction. The *story* is what matters. Manipulate the facts. Manipulate the characters. Manipulate and manipulate until the story *works*.

Here is my published story, which shed its original title of "What Does Your Father Do?" and became, for reasons of immediacy, "Your Father and Mine."

---

## *Your Father and Mine*

My father's doing it again. I think it, but like always, I don't actually say anything.

"What's the problem," I say.

Of course he says nothing. Like it's too difficult for him to tell me all the methodology that goes into fisting back the bay window's curtain with one hand, snapping off the lamplight with a twist of the other, and, I'm nearly positive, peering through his one good eye out into the crimes of the night.

I sigh. First like a sigh, then again more audibly, heavy with my chest and nose. Nothing. We live on a cul-de-sac in the middle of nowhere in particular. It's 10:00 p.m. and my mother is already asleep. She's smart enough to miss the nightly show. Not me. I want to know just what it is he sees out there.

"What's out there?" I say.

A grunt. Not even audible. Just a turn of his shoulders, the blue flannel inching back away from the light of the street. This is why I'm home? This is why I rushed back the moment

I took my last spring final? It went like this. Last weekend my mother calls me up, Sunday, and she makes small talk. You can tell when people make small talk by the way they don't hesitate between subjects. Like they're crossing items off a list. "Was there a lot of rain your way?" "Do you remember your grandma's birthday's coming up?" "Have you tried Ore-Ida's new twice-baked potatoes?" Then you get a pause and then the reason for the call. "I was at work the other night (my mom's a checker at the Safeway) and I got off at maybe eleven. So I'm driving home, this is Tuesday night so there's no real traffic, no bar traffic you know. So some car's making every turn I make. No big deal except it never happens. You know everyone in our neighborhood's retired. Except the Speare's and they never leave the house except to go to church. Even get their groceries delivered. So this car follows me right on up to our house. I park, and well I guess your father was looking out his window, you know, waiting for me. Well this car just pulls a little past me and just sits in the middle of the circle. Well your father comes outside with no clothes on, just his underwear, no shoes or socks on, just like you do—that's where you get it from. He says, 'Who's that?' and I say, 'Someone who followed me' and he says, 'What the hell for?' and I shrug and he starts throwing his arms around in front of himself and walking toward this car and he gets right up to it and whoever's in there tosses out a cigarette butt and then just takes off. So then your father gets in mine, it's still running and he takes off after this car. Well this car drives right through the vacant lot where the connector road's gonna be and your father slams on the brakes, reverses, parks, and gets out shouting, 'What the hell's going on, dammit!' So now he's in front of that window every night fully dressed with his car keys in his hand."

And here he is all right, peering out into the night with his one good eye. I told my mom, "He's been in front of the window ever since I can remember. I used to turn out my car lights before I hit our street just to freak him out. I'd walk up to the door all slow, or hide behind a bush, and he'd come out yelling, 'Who the hell's out here?' and I'd say, 'It's me, Dad. I'm looking for the cat.' And he'd say, 'stupid son-of-a-bitch' and he'd drag a hand across the hair on his chest and slam the door behind him. Then he'd pull out his keys and lock it. Just so I'd have to unlock it myself to get in."

She said, "That's not very respectful."

And I said, "Which part? Him locking it or me hiding from him?"

And she said, "Either one."

But the point is, he's always done this. I could never sit in the driveway with a girl and listen to the radio. Not that he wouldn't allow it, but he'd be looking at us, probably making sure no one was looking to harm us. Or maybe he'd just be looking.

He's what they call an International Counter-Intelligence Agent. Or what my mom calls a "high-ranking records officer." I call him a spy. Well, he was a spy. Now he's just, well, spying. He was a CIA man through and through. Right out of college.

So I say, "Maybe I'll go find Tiger."

My father sits down at this, less because I'm going out to get the cat and more because some stupid show just came on, one of those ones with the bike cops in spandex, and he sits forward under the lamp and rifles through the *TV Guide*. I step towards the door and without hesitation I turn to look at the floor between his chair and the table, looking more out of habit than curiosity, and sure enough, there is a scattering of colorful, cardboard squares lying one atop another leaking out in a trail to where the molding meets the floor. Advertisements for Hummel figurines, record clubs, Norman Rockwell collector's plates, and free book offers that my father has dutifully ripped away from the spine of every issue of *TV Guide* he's ever bought.

I asked him once, "You planning on joining all those record clubs?"

He'd answered back, "Does it look like I need to?" And with that he waved his hand in the direction of the entertainment center which, I noted, had again begun to collect the kind of brown dust I had never, ever, seen outside our house. "Dust's dust," I called it.

"No," I'd answered. "I guess four thousand albums are plenty." And I'd bet half of them were Elvis.

"I think I'll take a run," I say.

He says nothing as he reads, one hand spreading out the listings, the other poised on the remote. As I leave, snippets of dialogue about murders and car crashes fill the air. Outside I close my arms around me with a shake. It's spring but it's early spring, and getting dark, and looking back diagonally through the bay window, I can see the backward images of the television illuminating the window glass. When I was young I used to sit with my Legos, facing away from the TV, away from my father, but I'd watch what he watched through the reflections in the glass that framed our family portraits all across our living room. I saw everything he did, even if I did see it all backwards.

I know the cat is more than likely stalking moles in the vacant lot and I call out "Tiger" only to hear my voice. It's a beautiful night. The sky is clear and the moon has receded into a corner, opening up the stars and the faintest wisp of milkiness between them.

Nights like this my father and I used to sit outside well past my bedtime, my mother cajoling my father about my sleep patterns, my father telling her "The boy wants to listen to the ball game, the boy listens." So he would pop metal rings off beers and I would look up into the night sky through empty green-tinted Coke bottles, one for each eye like field glasses, and we would sit there silent, except for the shuffling of our feet and hands, and a baseball game would float in over our big wooden A.M. radio. Sometimes the Orioles, or the Phillies (Mike Schmidt was a "man" my father always said when he'd hit one out for the Phils), whatever would come in clearly, and

I would think of how one day, I would be able to keep my eyes open until the final out of the final inning.

We don't watch baseball together these days. Actually, we never watched together. We always seemed somehow more comfortable together outside in the dark of night. The weird thing is, I kind of think we wouldn't mind *listening* to a game, but that seems pointless when the games are all coming in on the TV. Besides, that wooden A.M. is long gone, and I just can't picture propping ourselves up on lawn chairs out back, cranking up the A.M. on my hundred-watt boombox, or sliding up and down dad's car radio dial to find some two-bit ballgame. I could just *see* that, my father and I in the front seat of his LeBaron, with him in his underwear, the keys already in the ignition, turned to full power, and him just poised for action.

And hell, the last time I asked my father to do something with me, maybe shoot some hoop, all he said was "What the hell for?" Clear enough. But a night like this gets you thinking. There's just all that space up there, space and blackness and it gets you thinking. When we were younger, before all these TV channels and computers and all, my father and I were never inside. My mother would come out and yell for dinnertime and we would both hear her but we acted like we couldn't. I always felt like those moments we spent after she called, the sun pushing west of us, were even more alive. They seemed to heighten my senses, and my father's, and no matter what we were doing, it seemed like the *only* thing to be doing.

I walk over to the center of our front yard and look in again. My father has found what he wants to watch, at least until the next commercial, and he's leaning back in his chair, and I look closer at his face, and I'm not sure why I'm searching, but I am, and the thing is, I can't see a smile. I've never seen him smile, at least outside of old photos. And it strikes me then that even in my deepest memories I can't see him smile, even from those moments in the gloaming, and yet I have seen clearly so many portraits in the house: me, Mom, and Dad all down at Sears in our finest clothes, with a stranger telling us where to put our hands, and we were always smiling.

There's a sweeping against my bare legs and I drop my head from the window to see Tiger has just passed under me. He turns and walks back through like I'm some great proscenium arch and I reach down to stroke his fur, right at the base of his spine where he likes it, and he lets out a little tweeting sound and makes his way up onto the porch. He's rubbing everything now, marking his territory: the corner of the top stair, the iron boot scraper, even the tins that hold peanuts and birdseed. Then, he pushes at the door with the arc of his back and his tail plumes up and with a tilt of his head he knocks the flashlight off the porch and into the flowerbed.

I come towards him and with a flip of his tail he turns and trots away. I pick up the flashlight and point it to check if it still has power, and the light circles around and seizes Tiger for a moment, and then he is gone. And I am reminded suddenly of flashlight tag. A torch of memories fills my head and they are overwhelming, and I suddenly wonder how the hell I have kept from remembering the countless nights my father and I spent playing flashlight tag in this yard, and out back, and in the nearby fields.

Clear nights such as this were always when we played. Dark enough for the flashlight to create an effect, with just enough moon to keep you running safely. Looking back now, the memory of this game seemed to always end with us flashlighting each other at the same instant. Undoubtedly, my father had always found me and withheld his burst of light until he heard the plastic sound of me fumbling to slide forward the big white switch. But now I place the flashlight back on the porch, with the beam shining a large circle on the door and I step back. And before I've even thought any of this through I walk up to where the window begins, just to the side and I start making loud noises in my throat. Garbled words in a voice I hope he won't recognize and while I call out to him I reach my hand to the window and extend my fingers like a cat's paw and just as my throat cuts off,

I scrape my nails along the glass and the wooden windowsill below.

Inside I hear thick noises, the slam of his chair against the wall, or maybe the toppling of his little lamp table. I have roused him. And for a moment I think of standing there, of coming clean. Or of telling him the damn cat was crawling along the window again, but I hear the flush of the front door opening and I duck down, pulling myself to the ground and his voice calls out "Who the hell is out there?" and I crawl under the porch, back under the front of the house behind a brick support. I reach my head around just a little, just to where one eye can see the break of the house. There is a light, a beam that seems too strong to be the flashlight I have left for him and my pupil recoils at this and I pull back again to hide. My eye stings a bit. Things are graying around the edges. I close it and open it again. I listen for his movement, knowing he will probably pull back for a moment to think. And after the space of ten, fifteen seconds, I hear the snap of twigs faint in the distance and as I peer out I see a sweep of light moving furiously around the yard, moving up out of my sight and then down again, toward the driveway and the cars, and then it sweeps across to the porch.

He begins to mumble and I make out pieces of what I know to be "stupid sons of bitches" and "who the hell's there?" and after a moment I'm not listening for the words, only for the source, and he is far now to my left, to the driveway and I get to my hands and knees and angle out right, out towards the front porch. It's slower, crawling out so noiselessly, but I am under the porch in a few seconds and I slide my arms out and pull myself up head first, and my eyes break the surface to see the silver flashlight I left for him is still there, pointing dimly into the empty living room.

I turn my head side to side to look for him, but I know he must be checking the garage, sweeping his bright Coleman torch across our abandoned bikes, our boxed-up board games.

*Stratego, Life, Monopoly, Twister.* I think of just shutting off that flashlight, replacing it, going inside to sit like nothing is nothing. And I'm still picturing this, trying to form the words he would say when he came back in, as my hand reaches hold of the flashlight and with a whirl, I'm off towards the woods. Towards the graft of the coming connector road, my feet pounding hard against the open black street. The moon is getting larger, and it moves in and out of my vision as I run. There's so much light as I edge into the field that I can make out the occasional mole scurrying from my path. I wonder if this is how a hawk sees, even in the pitch black of a new moon night, its yellow eyes like tiny bulbs shining on the spines of its prey.

I've run far enough to lose most of my breath, and I know I've gone far enough to escape him. I know by the time I turn and walk all the way back home my father will have made his way back in, found a new show to watch. Maybe even passed out for the night, the TV still flickering, audible. I put my light on to look for my footing, something I hadn't given a thought to as I ran. I can hear my heart, my breathing, the quickness of my blood. And then for a moment everything goes an orange-red, like coming back out of a deep sleep, and I feel like I'm fainting. And every time I've ever fainted comes back to me, too many times to remember clearly, but my father is there pointing at me, making remarks under his breath, and my mother is crouching down by my side, pressing a cold compress into my forehead, telling me he doesn't mean to be derisive, that he isn't really belittling me but that he's scared, she says, and I tell her it's just my diet for wrestling, I'm trying to cut weight and I'm low on iron, a slight nitrogen imbalance is all it is. Then I realize I'm not down, I haven't had a fainting spell. My pupils are warm with their adjustments, and in the distance a very strong light is aimed right at them.

My father is running toward me, his one free arm flailing and making a fist, his other hand perfectly steady on the Coleman. He's yelling "I see you. I see you. You son of a bitch I can see you." For a moment I think he must not know it's me, but then I think I've always been a son of a bitch to my father, and I start to seriously wonder if he even knows what it means to say that to someone. I think to yell back "Over here Pop. I saw the guy over here." And just then, the moment I've flipped the switch on my flashlight, a car door slams somewhere in the distance behind my father, and he stops short, and wheels around. Before I can make out what is happening my father has changed directions and is shouting again "You stupid son of a bitch."

I'm coming as fast as I can but my father reaches our street first. I strain to keep my neck steady as I run, pumping my fists in the air, the flashlight dropped somewhere behind me. My father has approached a man under the circle of light at the end of our cul-de-sac. He's a large man, a half a man bigger than my father. I can hear their voices, not the words but the sounds in their throats growing louder. When my feet reach pavement, the man puts my father in a half-Nelson headlock. He does it with ease, and I can see the stretch of muscle flex and ripple across his bare forearm.

For a moment neither of them says anything. They both stare at me, and it all looks so real that it seems fake. Staged. I half wonder if it isn't a friend of my father's or a new neighbor I haven't met, but then, with a slight movement they are in the light again, and across the man's hand there is blood. I think to say "unhand my father" but it sounds wrong, even now, and so I say nothing. I lower my head and rush right at them, hoping to put the crown of my head into this man's solar plexus. Hoping he'll drop right to the ground, and hard. My head hits another head, the raw, hollow sound is familiar. And I feel myself drop to the ground. From the pavement, looking up, I see the open mouth of the man, but there's a sharp ringing in both my ears, and at first I think I've hit his head and he's screaming out in pain. And then he lets his arm go and my father drops to the ground. It's my father's head I've hit and one ear opens up, then the other, and this man's laugh invites itself in and fills my head. It's in my neck too, my chest, my legs. I look over at my father and he gives me a look I can't make out. They say a boxer gives off every possible expression there is in the course of a fight, and I watch as my father's face says to me *you idiot, isn't this a bitch? kill this guy, will you?* and then *I love you, son*. It's at this point I know I'm delirious. My wrestling coach always called it the competitive high, that you break through the pain and go into a zone. But I feel more like I've just fainted again, only this time I've taken my father with me. And I'm just floating on the pavement and this man's laugh starts to come back up from my feet where it has landed, and then it's in my torso, in my gut, and it kind of settles there and I turn my head to get sick, but I haven't eaten and I just manage a cough.

And then it hits me, this man is the man who has come for my mother. He's the son of a bitch who followed her. He's the reason I'm lying on the pavement, a lump the diameter of a bar coaster growing on my forehead. He's the reason my father is out here in his underwear. Then I'm upright again, and my father's voice says "I never did see you wrestle." My chest moves out ahead of me and then my feet follow behind. I'm flying through the air, my hands and arms coming around like giant claws and then we're down, this man's bare back beneath my chin. I pull his arms up, one at each side behind him. I leverage my body and his with my legs and twist and I've got him pinned, both blades to the ground and I hold him there and the lights are already on us, and until I hear the metal sound of the handcuffs I'm unaware of the police. My father is pulling me up and from the corner of my eye I realize the light has come from behind me, from inside our house, and my mother is there, crying, her hand cupped to her mouth.

The police are saying something about the man to my father, something I can't quite make out, and an ambulance driver gives me a cold pack and tells me to call should I get

> dizzy again. My mother tells us to come in, that we should sit down and maybe eat something. But everything is a little fuzzy, a little quick. And I think to tell her no and then my father will say no, and then we'll say that we're not coming in now, that we're going to stay outside and maybe catch a ball game or take a drive or have a beer or two. And my father passes in front of me and looks at me, he is looking at me with *every* expression at once again, and his forehead is swollen and colored, and he says, "You really are one stupid son of a bitch. You know?" And I press a little more on the ice pack against my forehead and I look him dead in the eye and I say "I know, dad. I know."

---

One thing I've noticed over the years is that because I am so willing to let my characters evolve, and so desirous of telling a story, my father characters skew more negative and more actioned than my father ever was. And that is okay. When I was young, I wrote far too many stories—the kind I often see from students—wherein nothing much actually happens.

I was once on a full scholarship at Bread Loaf Writers' Conference and an editor of a top literary journal had lunch with me. She had obliged to read my two newest stories for possible publication. Having complimented me on my writing, she told me she liked one better than the other and was going to publish it. She had a sharp wit and a sharper tongue and remarked that she was accepting the one over the other because "At least something truly happened."

That forever drove home the reality that my characters must become their own people, make their own mistakes, and should not be constrained by whomever or whatever first inspired them. I rewrote the other story until something happened, and published it as well.

While my father may have inspired most, if not all, of my father characters, they do not resemble my father when they are completed. Some of his essence is there—quite a bit, actually—but my father was more beta than alpha, and I tend to write a more alpha father character in my fiction.

In my fiction-writing classes, I often remind my students not to release the tension in a story. In other words, *let your characters make mistakes.* Let them make choices that surprise you. Let them go. *Let the tension exist.* We are forever trying to release tension in our real lives, but in a story, you must not do this, or at least not until the story nears its end.

# —4—

# Your Dialogue Already Exists

## *And why listening to TV can help*

Obviously, the best way to learn dialogue is to read, and I will continue to speak on behalf of increasing your reading. Read quality, not quantity. Reread a page that teaches you.

But there are other ways to study dialogue, and a few of these have greatly benefitted my dialogue writing over the years. All of these came to me through my life. No one ever told me to do these things. They have come in an organic fashion, even though they may seem odd to you at first.

The first is to read plays, and attend plays, or even act in or rehearse plays. So many of the great dialogue writers end up in the theatre. Having held the lead part in every play my schools put on from fifth grade through seventh, I learned a lot by speaking great dialogue over and over again as I rehearsed. This led me to seek out and read great dialogue in plays and teach them as well.

Because I also teach film, and because I know people access film more often, I would argue this is the more likely genre to study. Because I happen to be an aesthete geared toward visuals, I often lose the thread of dialogue when I watch a film. I love the cinematography too much to gear my attention toward dialogue.

Because I have a large yard to mow, and because I am too stubborn to buy a riding mower, I have over the years taken to replacing my no-noise headphones with wireless headphones. This keeps me from getting bored, as the lawn takes well over an hour to mow.

One summer I realized that if I listened to a film, or more so, a great TV drama series on my headphones, I had to pay attention to the dialogue. Over the years I came to realize that if the film or TV show was one I had seen several times, and I could envision the characters and settings, I could truly focus on how the dialogue fit the character and story. Each time I mowed, I listened hard to the way the dialogue was crafted. I spent hours each summer listening to dialogue, mowing away, learning how to write, and envisioning my characters as actors.

These methods continue to drive home the fact that all of your characters need to exist in such a way that someone inhabits them, or in the case of actors, could inhabit them.

Good dialogue can actually carry and advance your story rather than simply be a function of necessity. Though I seldom begin a story with dialogue, I have noticed how often my students do, and so here is an example of how to open with dialogue. The characters must have singular voices, and their worldview must be present in what they say. But again, try to create a world along with the dialogue rather than just beginning with an unknown person speaking.

This story excerpt uses dialogue to develop the characters and advance the story itself:

---

## *Learned in the Home*

Bill put down the empty beer can and looked up at his wife, Jenna. He watched as she shifted the baby from arm to arm.

"The thing is," Bill said, "if Freud and those other damned doctors are right, well then that baby's already accumulated his notions about the world."

"I don't know," Jenna said. She placed the baby down and extracted a pack of cigarettes from the breast pocket of her shirt.

Bill watched her light up and toss the match toward their single-wide. He began to say something to her, stopped himself, and reached into the bucket for another beer.

"Jackasses," he finally said. "All of them."

Now that the sun was fully up, it wouldn't be long before her parents dropped by for their weekly Sunday visit.

"You know Bill, it would be nice if *your* parents came to see the baby sometime."

Bill spread his legs so that the baby could crawl under his lawn chair.

"Yeah, I know," he said. "You think I don't think about that most every day of my life? They won't travel up here, and I'm sure as hell not driving down I-95 through Portland and Boston with a screaming baby just to see them."

"I know," she said.

"And New York City too," he said.

"And DC," she said.

"Enough," he said. He bent over and placed his head upside down to look at the baby. Then he said, "You better not be putting those six-pack rings in your mouth."

•••••

It was noon before Jenna's parents showed up. As always, they had brought grocery bags full of dry goods from the Walmart in Houlton. Jenna's father carried them as far as the porch, and as the two women made their way inside, he took up his usual place next to Bill.

"Nice day," he said.

"Better be," Bill said, "because when these two or three weeks of fall are up, we'll be right back to seven months of winter."

"Lot of people were out driving around, looking at the leaves. So that's why we're a little late getting here today."

"I hadn't noticed," Bill said. "Have a beer?"

"No, thanks. We won't be staying long."

For a time the two men sat there staring off into the sun, thankful the other wasn't talking. They could hear Jenna and her mom inside putting cans away in the cupboard. After a few minutes, they came out, each carrying a tray of hors d'oeuvres.

---

I think it may be tone that most matters in dialogue. The kind of words used and the syntax together create tone, but so does the same combination in the surrounding narrative. One way to create tone in dialogue is to rely on the surrounding narrative and the actions depicted in that narrative to ratchet up the tension. In the above sample, the dialogue itself is doing the work, but the next example puts some of the onus on the surrounding narrative. Note the thick tension and how it is created in this section of my story, "Runaway." Pay attention especially to the father's diction, pace, and abruptness, as well as the surrounding narrative:

---

It was more than a week after our brief dinner conversation that he even said two words to me.

I was in the shower when it happened. He came in and he took a piss and then he put the lid down and sat on the toilet. I stood a half a foot back from the shower expecting him to flush it, but he only sat there, his face in his hands. When I finally stepped out he handed me a towel and watched me as I dried off and combed my hair.

"You aren't shaving yet, are you?" he said.

"No," I said, though I had been shaving under my nose for about a year. My father had more than once spoken of ungroomed facial hair as a weakness. I didn't really know what he meant by that, but I knew enough not to let him spot that weakness on me.

"Look, Jake. I want to ask you a question and I want you to answer me." He flushed the toilet and looked up at my reflection in the mirror.

"Okay," I said. I put my clothes on and used a hand-towel to dab at the counters where I had dripped.

"Did you, did Mom ever leave before?"

"How do you mean," I said. It was a phrase he hated and one I seldom used. For some reason, it came out then.

"When I was gone," he said. "At sea."

"No."

"Did you two ever leave?"

"You mean to take trips?"

"You know what I mean, Jake," he said. He banged on the side of the commode. "This damn thing," he said.

"I don't know what you mean," I said.

He stood up, lifted the tank lid and looked into the workings of the toilet. It was making a metallic, hissing sound.

"I mean, Jake, did you two ever leave with the intention of not coming back."

"No," I said. Then without thinking I said, "Only Mom's jokes about going to Vegas." I couldn't see his face, and I didn't need to. I was putting one and one together for myself. I felt a sense of relief in knowing where she was. I figured she'd be back when she ran out of money, or got sick of the people or the endless neon lights.

When my father turned around he was still holding the ballcock. "Fix this damn thing," he said. He slammed the bathroom door as he left, and in a minute I heard the sound of his car starting up. It was the last time I saw him for over a month.

---

In this scene you have just read, notice that the dialogue is deepening the characters and the reader's understanding of them, but the dialogue is also part of a real world of actions. Finally, notice that the dialogue is advancing the narrative action as well. When the father says, "This damn thing" and "Fix this damn thing" he is not simply talking about the toilet but about the family dynamic. It is no accident that this dialogue scene takes place in the bathroom so that the dialogue can take on the action and setting of the character's real world.

Your characters do not, or should not, converse in a vacuum. The real world must continue to exist, and because it exists, the real world can be utilized and thus incorporate the dialogue.

In my over twenty-five years of teaching, I believe dialogue has been the one element that vexes and truly frustrates students. Most students fall into one camp or the other. Either the student feels, correctly or incorrectly, that they are not good at dialogue, so they avoid writing dialogue…or the student believes, correctly or incorrectly, that they are good at dialogue, so they write too much dialogue into their stories.

Two points: The first is that when you are just starting out, dialogue is very hard to master. You should assume this will be one of the last elements, not one of the first elements, where you will find a high level of success. It follows then that you should not overdo the amount of dialogue in your story. The second point is that all elements should be used in service of the story. I rarely read a student story wherein the student has overused setting or overused plot.

Why is dialogue overused? Whereas underuse is related to a desire to avoid a difficult element, overuse is a product of two things. First, dialogue *seems* easy to write, mostly because it takes up page space quickly, *and* anything a character says seems fair game because we believe it is given from that character and therefore that character is giving their viewpoint. The problem with that thought process is that *all dialogue* should attempt to advance the story and/or deepen our understanding of the characters. Without that, the dialogue is simply robbing the reader of time to do these things, and the story is often left rudderless and shallow.

Second, we write too much dialogue because we read too much dialogue. If you read too much work by lesser writers, rather than professional writers, you are likely to encounter dialogue-heavy stories. In addition, too many writing students read young adult fiction and other genre fiction, which can be quite dialogue heavy. So, even if your goal is to write stories that are heavy on dialogue, and there are great ones, it is wise to *read* and *hear* quality dialogue so that you can begin to understand how it is done and how much dialogue you should write. Begin to discern the quality of what you are reading, whether it sold copies or not. You are learning the dialogue element itself, so you should only focus on the dialogue.

At the very least, as you get started, try to avoid opening or closing your stories with dialogue, and try to notice the ratio of dialogue to narration as you write. There will be certain stories where you will want more dialogue, but it should not be a default position. Let your reader learn something about setting, or better yet, character, before you plunge too deeply into dialogue.

A few writing details:

- Try to use *said* as your primary dialogue tag. This forces you to work hard in the dialogue itself rather than rely on an adverb in the dialogue tag ("She said sarcastically" is weak, her dialogue being sarcastic is strong).
- When a new speaker speaks, it is usually better to start a new paragraph.
- Try not to use exclamation points.
- When you use a question mark, use *asked* instead of *said.*

# — 5 —

# Your Style Already Exists

## *But here are some tools*

Essentially, every time you tell a story, you are telling it the way you want to tell it. Think of that *one* listener you have in your life who actually listens—does not interrupt you, and seems interested in listening to your stories (even if that person is you).

*That* person is who you are writing to. Now, you feel relaxed. You feel able to tell your story how you want to tell it.

Each story brings out a different mood in you, which means you use a different diction and syntax.

In large part, you tend to use the diction that comes naturally to you while fitting the story at hand. This is the same for syntax or the way you put the words of the story together. Sometimes you feel like using a rambling sentence when you tell your story. Sometimes you want quick bursts. Most times you want to be specific in detail, and sometimes you don't.

You are a natural storyteller. Trust your natural ability to tell your story.

Pick words that fit the emotion. Find your natural pace.

Get to the point, but let yourself meander when the meandering creates atmosphere or tension. And, because you are writing, take out all the *ums* and *you knows* and other stuff you don't need. Tell the story in the way you would want to hear it told to you.

Here is an excerpt from the same story used in Chapter Four, "Runaway," and it shows as close as I can show on paper how I speak in real life—if my speech were cleaned up and delivered slowly, with real thought, which is after all the point of taking the time to write. In other words, I try to write like I think, when I am alone and thinking slowly and carefully.

---

> When my father and I came home we noticed a few things missing: my mother's truck and her record collection among them. I had, of course, risked driving to the jail on just my learner's permit. I expected my father would ream me for it, but he didn't say a word. When he came out of the station he got right into the passenger side. The only thing he said to me was "stay there." So I drove home, well under the speed limit, half expecting to be smacked upside the head for driving his cherished 1972 Chevy Nova.
>
> The next day he went into the attic and pulled out the boxes of records I guessed had belonged to him before they'd gotten married. Buddy Holly, Elvis, Eddie Cochran, Chuck Berry, Les Paul. There were some other records too, mostly on drumming techniques, and what must have been country and western. Records with names like Buck Owens and Roy Clark, people I'd never heard of. He put them into the empty built-in shelves where my mother's records had always been. For years, my mother had listened only to dance music. Waltz, Bosa Nova, Flamenco, it didn't matter as long as there were steps she could learn. She would order the plastic templates of the steps from the back of the albums or make them herself out of yard-sale Twister games. She would learn each dance to the point of perfection—and *always* by herself. My father had banged his knee on a door shaft in a submarine years back, and couldn't, he said, take the stress of dancing. He had served tours on practically every type of vessel known to man, supported operations all around the world, even taken fire atop

an aircraft carrier—and yet his lone injury came from stumbling around a sub after an all-night peace-time poker game. It was the one endearing thing about my father.

That first night we spent alone he put a stack of maybe six of his records onto the turntable and lit a cigarette. He watched me eat the last of the apple pie Mom had baked the day before she left.

---

Think of your narrative writing as the best version—but a real version—of how you speak (or rather, would speak if you had the time to do so carefully) to an attentive listener. The same holds true when writing in third person.

Here is a third-person narrator in an excerpt from my story "The Clipping of Maynard Jax" within which you can clearly recognize my voice. You can recognize my voice because I am writing as close as I can to the way I speak, or at least, how I think I would speak if I slowed down and took my time:

---

And it's highly unlikely that Maynard thought to himself how he was kind of in a circle himself. Fact is—and that's what papers are notorious for caring about, though they seldom seem to possess them—Maynard stood still like a pole, like the sharp end of a compass, and around him you might have drawn a circle. Behind him the river was just beginning to crack. It was at least a month ahead of the norm. Everything about that river was off that day. What should have been ice was water. What should have been still was already in motion. Some force pushing the breaks of ice along in slow, but chaotic paths. The berms aside the river serving as bumpers. This rushing sound was behind him, a kind of monotone beneath the crackling and bumping. And above Maynard was the constant sound of aircraft. What the paper might have mentioned was

> that this bar, this establishment was only two miles from the Air Force base. The flight path did not include this section of the river, but did encompass areas directly north and south, stretching to the outskirts of Twin Forks, into the homesteads and farms beyond.

---

In writing dialogue, the same holds true, except the fact that you want to write how *each character* would speak. This, again, is why I like to base my characters in real people and then manipulate, add, and subtract. If you do not do this, all of your dialogue will sound like the same person: you, the writer. The narrative voice can be based on you even if that is the narrator. The characters in the story cannot be based on you, though there will be a way into them—a familiarity from real-life people—so that you can play their part and see the world as they do.

This creates one issue, which is the third-person narrator (likely based on your way of thinking/speaking) sounding exactly like the main character (based on your way of thinking/speaking). You do not want that.

Such an issue was at hand for me when I wrote a story called "Gestures" which was published in *South Dakota Review*. In order to pull off that story, I tried to make the conversations brief. Even when writing longer exchanges, I tried to make the lines quick, to the point, and very matter-of-fact. This allowed me to use my more natural speaking voice in the third-person narrator, as I do when I write mostly in first person. The narrator, even now as a third-person non-character, is where my normal speaking voice resides. The main character of the story is revealed through the third-person narrator voice, which is my natural voice. Thus, the main character, Daniel, is assigned a matter-of-fact dialogue voice, which keeps it from blending with my narrator's voice.

You might ask: Why, then, did I not write the story in first person, since my artistic belief and methodology seems to suggest I choose first person for every story? The answer is that this story concerns the death of the main character's father. I believed that as the writer, and certainly for my readers, taking out the linkage and assigning the storytelling to a third-person narrator tamped down the maudlin aspects—or worse, dreaded sentiment—I strive to avoid in all my short stories.

Here is an excerpt from "Gestures" that exemplifies all this discussion:

---

It occurred to Daniel that he had now been living in Denver for thirteen years and he hadn't a clue what the local newscasters looked like. He had grown up with his father in Fargo. Lived there his whole life before moving to Denver to work construction. His father had said, "Why don't you build things here?" Daniel had answered there wasn't enough work. And it was true. Fargo was too cold six months a year to work outside anyway. In Denver, he was known to say, two days of snow brings two days of sun. Usually, he was right.

"You want sound?" Doris asked. She was talking over her coffee cup. The steam seemed to come from her mouth as she spoke.

"Just weather," Daniel said. "Snow, I'm sure."

"I bet it stops," Doris said.

Daniel started to think of the winter sun in Denver. And then Doris said, "Eventually."

"You're a funny lady Doris," he said. He came over to where she leaned on the counter.

"Here," he said. "You can have these." He held out the Styrofoam plate of bagels and cheese.

"Thanks," she said.

"On my tab," he said. "I'll get you that money when I get back to Denver. Promise."

Doris turned up the TV sound and took a bite. "Sure," she said. "I know you're good for it."

Daniel ducked into the bright corridor. From behind, he heard the weatherman say the snow was dissipating. "Sure," he said. "Sure."

Daniel took his usual seat in the lobby near the fountain. It was a statue of a saint. It looked as if it had once been copper in color. The head was still a golden brown. The body, where sprays of water found temporary and consistent perch, were streaked with green and black. It might once have been a specific saint. Now, he thought, it could be any saint. Maybe that was best. People could sit under the lull of the fountain and pray as they liked. For a moment Daniel wished he was with a church. He had often sat in this place, the mist of the fountain kissing his face, and thought about what lacked in his life. He had no money. No insurance. After more than a decade he was still doing the same jobs. Laying paper and shingles perched on the roofs of homes of people that would never know his name. Laying brick for outdoor barbecues. He had no wife. No children. His longest relationship had been less than a year. He thought, if I could just make my way over to the hospital's chapel, I could pray for him. But he knew it wouldn't help. He worried that his very presence in the hospital carried some kind of negative force. He had never helped his father in a way he could remember.

He phoned Stacie.

"I'm not helping," he said.

"Oh, Daniel. I know. I feel so helpless too. Do you want me to come out again. I could get Pam or Mrs. Atkins to sit the kids."

"No. Stacie. No. I'm just saying what's the use. I can't do anything. I feel like an undertaker here."

"I know."

Daniel twisted the metal pay phone coil in his fingers. "I shouldn't have called," he said. "I know you're busy. How are the kids?"

"Good. They're good." He could hear her blow smoke into the receiver. "They're starting to ask questions about Grandpa. You know, when is he going to call they ask. Stuff like that. I don't know what to tell them."

"What do you tell them?'

"I tell them he's sick. I tell them he sleeps a lot. That he needs his rest."

"He's been sleeping alright," Daniel said in a low voice. "He's been sleeping for more than six weeks."

He told her he'd call again and hung up. The phone swallowed the quarter. Daniel hated the way Stacie had sounded. It was as if she sensed the day had come. She had never sounded so fearful, he thought, in her whole life.

---

The final fiction element to note is pace.

The biggest error my students make is rushing their work. Time, fear, and many other factors cause this rush. The way to think about this as you write is to ask yourself: Which parts would be interesting to my readers if I slowed down and gave more detail? Which parts would be better if I used a bit more summary? Think about the way you tell your friends or family a story. You slow down and speed up because you know what parts are going to be most interesting. You know this because the story already happened, and so you know what parts are interesting to you. So, in a story, think as you write. Is this an interesting part? Should I slow down and detail? Trust yourself, and always rewrite with an eye on pace.

# POETRY

# — 6 —

# Your First Line Matters

## *And so does your title*

Poetry is not as hard as fiction writers think it is, but it is a different animal. Most student writers simply write very short or overly long lines, throw in a rhyme scheme, and end on page one. This chapter, instead, will guide you toward the writing of literary-journal-quality poems that work, and the work itself will be easier than writing fiction. And, in some ways, more difficult... Poems are short, and that requires efficient writing, but they are also capable of achieving depth. And that is where the difficulty lies. At once, a poem's title can be efficient and yet unforgettable. The title can be a microcosm for the poem itself.

Let us work with my poem "Fontanel" and look closely at its measured efficiency, and its depth. I like to think of the title as an orienting response opportunity. I have long been fascinated by that hindbrain response we have when we see or hear or smell something. When a student arrives late to my class, everyone notices, and they are reoriented by this change. No one keeps studying what I have written on the board. This is normal and part of how we have evolved. Because we need orientation, and because people can't help but read your title, why not use your title to orient your reader?

The word *fontanel* may not be known by my readers, but it is the correct word for this context, and my hope is that by the end of the poem, my reader has a full understanding of the word, and thus the metaphor is properly driven home. It is a risk though, and one that must be contemplated. In general, you should use unusual words only when you feel the benefits outweigh the risks. Everything in writing should matter, but the title may matter the most.

---

## *Fontanel*

Under new-mooned summer evenings
I visit my father like sleep
to plead with him to open his bone-dead eyes,
"Here, look, your grandson."
I will place him in your arms,
hold him there for you.
Encircle your dead fingers,
across his temples.
Feel his pulse now.
Your death is like the soft chasm, there in front,
Within his growing skull.

---

We will work more with "Fontanel" shortly, but for now, here is another example of using the title to orient the reader. In my poem entitled "Highway Blueberries" I am able to move right into my details and let them accumulate, because I have used my title to properly orient the reader. It is of note that a title that orients should still, when able, be interesting on its own. In this case, it is an interesting title, and not one I had seen before. It came the way it should: organically. My family frequents a wonderful farm situated along a rural highway—or byway to some—and it always seemed odd to me to be doing this peaceful thing, picking blueberries, while dealing with road and noise pollution. In a sense, the title is the macro, and the poem is the micro:

---

## *Highway Blueberries*

Logging trucks hug the first row, spewing thick black smoke
Carcinogens like atoms, a DNA double-helix of death.
The fog collects like trash on the roadside,
Before organizing in uniformed teams to descend
On this acre of high-bush Maine blueberries. Families
Have assembled in cohorts of threes and fours, the Amish
The Lutherans and the Atheists. Children play chess
On the human sized board, watching, and pointing,
At the smoke as it dissipates, fallout falling in between

Row after row of green and blue berries. New buds mingle
With full, berries straining to be reached in the thickness
Of untrimmed hedgerows. The smoke settles into physical
Soot atop straw hats and fingernails, the berries loose
In hands, filling bags and the footfall below. No one picks
The fat blue berries nearest the road. Another logger rolls by.

---

Now, not only did the title orient my readers, but it allowed me to create a solid first line. If your title fails, you then spend your first line orienting the reader, which is often less successful if not a little clumsy. The last thing I want is stalled motion. An orienting title allows me to get up to speed quickly even in the first line, and that means the reader is propelled—and likely to read my poem in full—with anticipation.

Another title that helped me immensely was "How to Die Happy." This title came to me without a poem. I am sure I read it somewhere or heard it somewhere (you should always be ready to receive from the ether), and it just rolled around in my head. Death is a constant, and the idea that death and happiness can coexist is anathema to me.

So, naturally, deaths of relatives and friends started to attach over the coming days to the thought of dying happy. The title thus spawned the opening line of the poem:

"My grandfather died on New Year's Eve, 1962."

This line came to me because it is a fact. Death never has good timing, but some deaths are particularly awful. My grandfather died the evening my father proposed to my mother. Take that in for a moment. My father never told me this. I read it years after he died in my paternal grandmother's autobiography.

So, I could easily write that poem as it happened, but it is almost too sad to believe, so I never wrote that poem. Instead, the line appeared by writing down the title: "How to Die Happy." The second line also came easily:

---

## *How to Die Happy*

My grandfather died on New Year's Eve, 1962
After gorging on a tenderloin steak

---

My grandfather died of a heart attack, and I know from my grandmother's written recollection that he had eaten some meat beforehand. It was New Year's Eve, so perhaps a roast or duck or something of that nature. Steak is linked with heart issues, but even more so, my grandfather ran a small company for a time that delivered poultry and meat. I imagined a steak.

The next five lines finish the first stanza:

---

## *How to Die Happy*

My grandfather died on New Year's Eve, 1962
After gorging on a tenderloin steak
The kind he used to deliver
In a black and white panel truck
*Zuras Poultry & Meats* painted
In black & white or red white & blue.
Because he once was a marine.

---

Where did this poem come from, exactly? Well, I have seen a photo of my grandfather's meat and poultry truck. My grandfather was also a marine; thus, the patriotic paint scheme idea that came to me.

As you can see, this poem is a product of mining my past, which means mining everything that has affected me personally. This is my actual grandfather's death. His actual truck. And as you can see, only slight manipulations are needed. I find honesty more necessary in poetry than fiction, in the sense that while my stories are fictionalized, my poetry is more direct, informed by confession and catharsis.

Now, let's examine the second stanza of this poem:

---

In old photographs he seemed to enjoy
Living in his black & white world—
My Czech grandmother, his proud wife
Astride him, dressed to the nines
In the latest black and white flapper wear.

---

My grandmother was born in Czechoslovakia (as it was then known), and I have seen multiple photos where she was dressed in her everyday fashion as a flapper in her mid-twenties. All my grandparents now exist, (and for my grandfathers *always)*, as black and white photo participants. So, I over-emphasized black and white, but in this poem acted as if it was all real and true, and so it is not simply a poem about looking at old photographs.

Looking at photographs can be a great spark for writing poetry. It can be a poem about a single photograph, or a poem that comes from looking at several photographs. I also see memories as a type of photo collage.

In this poem, I was working from memories: photos I had seen, stories I had been told. In a sense, mining your past is a way of collecting and synthesizing artifacts, and a creation of art through the filter of memory and manipulation.

Here is the final stanza of the poem:

---

My mother's father never ate steak,  
Or at least not on the night he died.  
 (we never spoke of his death, only alcohol)  
In the lone photo I possess, he is in color,  
Smiling, his curly steel hook deep in ice,  
Hauling its weight on his back, upstairs.  
Upstairs, they await his arrival—  
Perhaps it is a penthouse apartment,  
Angels awaiting a block of ice  
To place in front of their fans.  
A velvet couch, my grandfather  
Reclining, the sweat on his lovely  
Brow dissipating into cool air.

---

At this point in the poem, I have introduced a companion subject by adding my maternal grandfather to the mix. The only photo I have ever seen with me and my maternal grandfather together was in color, an honest point of contrast to my black and white paternal grandfather. My mother's father did indeed haul ice to people's houses in the 1920s and 1930s, and I have seen such a photo. Alcohol enters the poem, also, out of truth.

Then, I introduce the *turn* of the poem, and often this is where manipulation comes into play. I am only imagining my grandfather in a penthouse apartment, replete with a velvet couch. What is happening in this *turn* and final image is that the title comes alive. Because I wrote this poem from a title that came to me, the entire time I was writing the poem, the idea of dying happy would have been always with me. My grandfathers were Catholic, and so naturally the world belonging to them was organic. I pictured the ice delivery as an ascension and tried to tie together the physical world and the spiritual world in an organic manner.

Here is another poem where the title and the first line are what made the poem take off:

---

## *Beauty*

Remember that early autumnal evening in Colorado
Still light with fireflies, the air warm and sticky,
The two of us waiting for a table at a steak joint
With the bourgeois of Denver? Faces pressed
To the shop-glass, the uninhabited sidewalk beckoning?

A shift of eyes, of bodies, pugnacious, and our group being
Found them—two beautiful women impossibly dressed,
Crossing the boulevard diagonally, their faces a shock
Of white-capped teeth and crimson lips, graceful,
Silence like a threat to our hungry eyes, bellies,

As if the streets had been shut down for filming.
Do you remember wondering why no one spoke?

It was as if we had witnessed something we did not
Understand, something not seen in the three dimensions
Of daily humdrum life. Beauty, undisturbed and obvious.

And then one man's voice, in a whisper: *call girls*.
The hungry faces now blank, somehow uglier with pallor,
envy. Two beautiful women on their way
In the falling night, their images lingering in stranger minds,
Ready to tear into flesh when their number is called.

---

This poem came about because one day, I remembered the vision of that event out of the blue. I imagined, in my voice, walking up to my wife and simply saying, "Remember that early autumnal evening in Colorado?"

Any reader can read my poem and imagine this situation. It may remind them of something similar, and/or it may at least ask them, or allow them, to contemplate my title—my notion, my idea, my question—of how we understand and confront beauty. Poets confront ideas as well.

Notice that I did not capitalize the word *envy* in a poem where I have chosen to cap all first-line words. Sticks out, sorely, doesn't it? Little so-called *tricks* or *tools* like this can do a lot of work for you if you use them *sparingly.*

This is a poem wherein I wanted, and thus composed, longer lines. The poem called for a contemplative voice so that the reader would truly slow down and consider the topic/event. If I had wanted to follow the eight-to-twelve syllable edict, I would have shortened the lines, not by removing words, necessarily, but through the reduction of longer words.

In truth, this is the easiest way to control the syllables in your lines. I could have removed the word "undisturbed" and replaced it with "alone" in the penultimate stanza. Think a moment, though, and note that the word "alone" has different connotations from the word "undisturbed." Either word could work, and it is a choice both of syllabic length *and* meaning, which therefore affects not only line length but rhythm. At the heart of every poem is not the line but the word itself. Everything begins with diction.

If you contemplate diction, you not only contemplate length and time and rhythm, but also alliteration and assonance and consonance. In other words, every letter and syllable will create something, just as every note or rest does in a musical work.

What about those long poem titles you occasionally see? How can you use them effectively?

When I studied poetry in my MFA program, I was living in the Deep South, and I found that Southern poets were particularly good at using long titles in poetry. I don't use them very often, but occasionally it fits the poem. Not only can a long title do some work for your poem, both orienting the reader and explaining the event, but such titles can be wildly interesting on their own. If such a title forms for you, be sure it works on all these levels: orienting the reader, explaining or suggesting the event, and interesting the reader enough for them to be unable to refuse reading the poem. Make sure the title fits the tone of the poem and is not used simply to be clever or different. You will know if you are being honest with yourself.

Here is an example of a long-title poem, with the title actually *working*:

---

## *Why I Write Poems While My Sons Rehearse Mumford & Sons*

My red dictionary
Is less beautiful than my youngest son's 1976 cherry-red
Lawsuit Ibanez Double-Axe: A 4-string bass atop
6-strings cuts through the bullshit. My Merriam
Dictionary entraps shit like Pandora's Box. My pen
Is not as mighty as his stainless-steel Geek Pick.
And my blurry-blue college-lined notebook looks *weirdly* elongated
Lined next to my oldest son's synthesizer keys.
His Moog, with its left-hand side wheels, *bends* notes
With ease, as I struggle to find a rhyme or litote.
Is it because when my sons are off rhythm or pitch

They simply backtrack and fix it?
They simply adjust and play correctly?
I erase a word, add another, a pink nubby
Eraser in my hand, a dulled number two
Ticonderoga in the other.

I tap along with their rhythm, easing from Bowie to
Mumford to Wilco. Switching from electric blue Yamaha
To GoodTime Banjo to acoustic Hummingbird.
Their music floats like ether, and I thrum, thrum, thrum,
To the staccato until my wife calls us all for dinner,
Her homemade aromas mixing with the notes in the air.

# — 7 —

# Writing Your Surroundings/Life

***And thus, even <u>this moment</u> becomes your past***

Here is an example of a poem that exemplifies writing from your life. I wrote this poem a day after my wife and I toured a house we were thinking of buying:

---

## *House Hunting*

The baby is riding my shoulders up high,
Jostling his hips and pointing wet fingers at the seller
As if she has something to hide

I'm pointing her way too,
In the basement where the bricks won't tuck,
In the corners where the floors divot and lean.

My wife glares at me and hugs her chest,
Like we better buy this one or else—

Maybe the antebellum plainness of it all?
The men and women who have wiled life here
Add up over time

Into nothing.

The baby resumes kicking my kidneys
While I rub windows for traces of heating oil,

And open the toilet tanks and skim for sediment,
Flip on the lights to check for electrical strains—
The baby reaching and pointing all the while.

My wife and the seller look like sisters,
Measuring the countertops and vaulted ceilings,
Like the movers are at the doorjamb.

The seller *mentions* her prostate cancer
As if she's pointing out a carpet stain.
My wife holds her at the wrist,

I think again, They could be sisters. . . .
"I thought only men contract that," I say.
"Some men get breast cancer," she replies.

I shift my weight over my heels,
Ask her to sign the disclosure form,
Mindful of the irony,
The growing weight on my back.

---

Carrying a baby around on your back while house hunting is a strange endeavor. It is like the reality of buying a house to raise children in is materialized for you. Every step, every attempt to climb a staircase, is magnified by the literal weight on your back.

What young poets do when faced by such an opportunity for a poem is to write, essentially, what I just wrote in the preceding paragraph. And that is fine in paragraph form, dead on and exact, as an exercise. In fact, I created that exact exercise and have occasionally assigned my poets the task of composing, sometimes before and sometimes after, a paragraph wherein they first say in plain English what they want to say in their corresponding poem. This works well for apprentice poets, and you often get quite decent poems out of the exercise, although they can still in their finished form be a bit didactic, a bit too on.

As you advance as a poet, you learn indirection. Such indirection is at work here in "House Hunting" and is only met with directness in the poem's final line. One of the main reasons we use indirection is that it allows us the opportunity to use sense details. The open secret amongst working poets is that details, and especially sense details, are what garner a poem's ultimate success. It is easy to teach, but hard to learn. The biggest reasons for this are, firstly, that young poets are not focused enough on the task at hand, and secondly, are fearful of choosing the correct details from an infinite number.

Let's face it: our culture is not one of noticing our surroundings. But if you are reading this book closely, that means perhaps you are someone willing and able to truly focus on details. So, we will deal primarily with the second reason: that of choosing the *right* details. Cliches are less helpful in our poems than in our songs. In poetry, we are expected to use the usual, fresh word. The way to find that word is to once again be organic. My title is "House Hunting" and my persona is in a house, looking closely at the house for possible purchase . . .therefore, as a poet, I use the actual moment. You can jot things down or simply recall as you write. It is the detail that accumulates and creates the basis on which you can get philosophical or, in a final line, provide a metaphor (which allows some head-on didacticism).

Before looking at houses, like most people, I read some advice online. So, the idea of looking for sediment and rubbing the windows came from reading advice, and though I did not actually do that when I was looking at houses, I remembered it for the poem. In addition, I had recently read an article pretty much by accident that discussed, confusingly for me, this notion of female prostate cancer. That line serves as the *turn* in the poem. From there, the poem can move away from the details because it has already *established* its foundation in a *three-dimensional world.*

Here is "Fontanel" again. Here, the *present* is mined. The truth of my life presented the opportunity for the poem and thus, for me, some catharsis. My father passed away before my sons were born. For the person who holds ownership of it, this fact constantly materializes in the real world. Here is another lesson in being an artist. Every single person in my shoes would have noticed the absence, but rather than immediately suppress such moments and bury them, thus actually feeling the pain more, the artist—in this case the poet, me, the persona—notes the moments and contemplates them in the subconscious.

When ready, the poet draws on the moment and creates the art—in this case a poem. Here is how this poem manifested:

---

## *Fontanel*

Under new-mooned summer evenings
I visit my father like sleep
to plead with him to open his bone-dead eyes,
"Here, look, your grandson."
I will place him in your arms,
hold him there for you.
Encircle your dead fingers,
across his temples.
Feel his pulse now.
Your death is like the soft chasm, there in front,
Within his growing skull.

---

The final line uses the metaphor set up by the title, but also indirectly discusses the problem: growing. A young poet might write, "My father will never see my son grow up" and then proceed down a list-path of things the son might do that the grandfather will miss. And that is not bad, it just is too *on*. Through indirection—by saying that my son's skull is growing and linking it to his grandfather's death—the reader makes the connections. Sometimes, readers untrained in poetry will be moved by such connections these lines make yet will remain unable to explain why they are moved. That is fine. Not all readers need to be trained to comprehend the writer's advanced poetics, but as poets, we need to be trained to create the poetics nonetheless. Read my poem a few times, then try to get it out of your head. Forgetting the poem will be made much more difficult because of the images, the word choices, the way it is phrased, and the way the connections work so deeply. That is the purpose of the writer: to create what continues to exist, even when the reader is finished with the work itself.

When my mother passed away, I drove my family eight hundred miles to her house in Virginia. I had not been inside my mother's house in years, as we tended to meet her for outings or, just as often, she would fly up to see us in Maine. When we arrived at my mother's house to clean it out, I had little understanding of what I would be entering into. The first thing I did was go inside by myself while my wife and our young sons stayed in our car in the driveway. I came back out shortly and confided this new reality I had discovered to my wife.

The following poem came directly from that experience seeing how my mother had been living:

---

## *Hoarding*

The yard should have been a clue, overgrown
Oak leaning on the roof, lazily,
The drainpipes clamming at the cornerstones.
Rainwater clearly finding purchase
In the drywall. An acre of land, once mowed,
Regressing back into a prehistoric hell.
The front door unable to perform its duty,

Unhinged, door-stopped by years of hoard.
The stench of Lysol masking mold and
Cat litter.

Outside you sat in the car, each of our two
Boys belted in from the 800-mile ride,
Their father inside a house they had seen
In photographs. Mom's house. Is it
The residue of a life spent that we discover
As we sift through sixty-eight years?
A world of possessions defiant, living
At our feet, above ground, unattached now
From meaning.

I stood there.

I knew in a minute I would have to let you in
To a world I had only myself discovered. Our boys
Exposed to the ravish of extended widowhood
Now three generations deep. Deep. Each room deep,
More deep than the next, in bubble wrap, empty
Cans, and piles of bee carcasses. A shattered window,
Poorly patched with cardboard, in the room I
Occupied. In her bedroom, past empty canisters
Of Lysol and unopened mail, chip bags, a box
Somehow empty save for a blanket scrap,
A stray cat that must have wandered in. Found a home.
The last known vestige of her life.

---

The detail at hand, the reality of the physical world: that is what carries the *weight* of the poem. Note the lack of sentimentality. Sentiment is the least convincing form of writing that has ever existed. Trust the physical world. Trust detail. Trust the use of language, the placement of words, the use of punctuation.

Catharsis is part of art. I have continued to use my present, and more so, mine my past for truthful material. This allows real and honest art and allows me to process my life. Here is the poem I wrote years before my mother's death, not long after she had recently mailed some of my deceased father's belongings to me:

---

## *First Christmas without My Father*

At Christmas each year, my father
produced the same ornament anew,
unlayering countless dusty-blue tissues
from an old shoebox lettered in black:
*Public Shoe Company*. This, he said,
was his father's. It was a P-47 Thunderbolt
with fraying tape across its wings.
And what I remember is not my father's
face, nor the care he must have taken
nor the timbre of his voice, but the way
the thin wing-tape contained several
narrow spines of string, for strength.

My father's Lionels arrived today.
My mother had no use for them anymore,
she wrote. And with that, she had boxed
the old three-railed silver tracks, the straights,
the curves, and the switches, and the individually
wrapped, interlocking railcars. My father's trolley
was there too, the type that lights up from inside,
casting shadows of men reading the daily news
with grim, morning faces, beneath worn,
checked homburgs. She'd send the village later,
she wrote, and had marked the box in black:
FRAGILE.

---

Again, it is in detail that a poem is made. It would be impossible to not understand and feel the *love* in this poem. It is the difference between being *told* something and being *shown* something. In other words, I am convinced of your love by being *shown* your love for me. When someone dies, we cling to that person's prized physical items. It is what we do.

In both of these poems, I honestly explore my situation at the exact moment. Rather than be macro and vague, I am micro and detailed. Rather than sentimental, the poems are logical. This is the key. The only way to actually move your reader is through actual details, which means actual things. Logic. Don't worry that emotion will not come through. It will. *Without sentimentality.*

This box of my late father's belongings arrived at my house unannounced and was actually marked *fragile*. Like any bereaved person, I opened that box, contemplated everything in the box, felt immense sadness, and was unable to shake the experience.

Every untrained poet, regardless of education and experience, can write that a death left them cold and lonely, and anyone can write that death is hard and dark and difficult. Those are abstract thoughts. In concrete detail is where you will find truth. It actually is those trains that make me connect with my father. It is that cat in my mother's house that my brother adopted after her death. Life is detail.

## — 8 —

# Free Verse Means Freedom

***Though your worldview remains intact***

Another way to understand freedom in poetry is the idea, taught by many poets, that there is an initial subject and then the actual subject. For some, that feels too much like trickery, and I understand that. Some see it as being misled or lulled into something that isn't the subject, then being given the subject, and that feels fake somehow. What I try to do in many of my poems is to close that gap. Because I write from my past—occasionally my just-passed-present moment, and sometimes from forming memories of my past as I write—I try to make the subject real from the beginning but then follow that subject even when it goes somewhere I had not planned.

I decided to write a poem entitled "Three Rolls-Royces" after realizing I had accumulated some brushes with the actual cars over the years. As I began the poem, I was working from a place of good feelings, and the poem was somewhat light in tone. I was open to discovering the actual subject, whatever that may be. As I wrote, I obviously got in touch with my humanness, and my somewhat impoverished upbringing, and without ever having planned it, envy reared its ugly head. The difficult thing, and what often separates art from commerce, or at least art from schlock, is brutal honesty. Most readers assume the poem's persona is that of the poet. Mostly, they are right, with a manipulation here and there. As that base emotion rose in me, I allowed it, even welcomed it, and wrote it to its completion. The poem did not entirely surprise me, because it is honest. The honesty is part of why it worked. However, if I had started out with such a theme of "envy," then my poem would have been shallow, didactic, trite even. Instead, I was quite pleased with the result, and it found its way to publication. Here is the full poem:

---

## *Three Rolls-Royces*

The first time we saw a Rolls-Royce
We were hand-in-hand, remember?
We walked Aspen, our first Siberian,
In summer heat, down to the First Baptist
Church, Charpentier Historic District,
South of I-10 in deep, deep Louisiana.

It was blue and white, or silver maybe,
Shining like an oiled-up hard-on,
Remember? I was teaching English,
So what choice did I have but to note
The irony of a Rolls-Royce at a Baptist Church. You said:
*My Uncle Jasper was a Baptist preacher in Mississippi.*
I wanted to sit on its hood and await the owner,
Remember? But Aspen tugged at her leash,
And it was hot, dead noon, Sunday.

The second time was in Presque Isle, Maine.
Right down the road from the three-story ramshackle
We rented. Aspen had died, replaced by Sasha.
The keys were in the Rolls, nighttime, dealership closed,
Like an unholy temptation. The price: two thousand dollars.
The grill intact, worth half that alone, the real wood
Dash waiting to be oiled, its aromas buried under dust.

We might have bought that Rolls . . . I said:
*Picture it: Everyone we know following us down*
*The street like a Mardi Gras parade. Me in a black*
*Top hat, you in a sash. What a sight we could be!*

The third time we were underground, submerged
In a mall in Washington, DC, remember?
Face deep in Asian noodles, some jackass
Was behaving like a jackass to a teenager
Working the till at Urban Outfitters.

When Jackass left,
I followed him into the parking structure
The next street over.
I don't know why
I followed him,
What I expected
I might do. When I came back
I never told you what happened:

Jackass was driving a black Rolls-Royce.
When he passed me by, I caught a glimpse
in a store window. For a moment it appeared
I was driving. What I never told you was:
I wished I were him.

---

Clearly, the jackass in the poem is me, isn't it? I mean why not rise above it all with some dignity? And why not realize money isn't everything?

And mostly in my real life I do, but I am imperfect and I have my moments, and so I allowed this persona and the Rolls-Royce cars to personify that moment of envy we feel but seldom reflect upon.

What was true and what was manipulated?

Well, the last bit is a representation of that envy. I never followed a

Rolls owner into a parking garage nor caught a glimpse of myself in a window driving, or seemingly driving, a Rolls.

But my wife and I did walk our dog Aspen past a church in Louisiana and wondered about the duality of attending a poor church in a shiny new silver-blue Rolls. We saw this same car at the same church most Sundays. I never forgot it.

Weirdly enough, there was a Rolls for sale in my northern Maine town more than a decade ago, and my wife and I did sit in it, and because it was so cheap, I did contemplate our buying and driving that 1980s Rolls. And Sasha was our dog's name at the time. As I write this, our dog Indigo is at my feet. Pets are the kind of detail that makes a poem seem real.

The imagined parade flowed from the first Rolls sighting in Louisiana, the state of parades. The parades I watched in Louisiana obviously helped set up, in my mind as I wrote, the idea of me driving the third Rolls.

I never *really* wanted to sit on the Rolls in Louisiana and await the owner, but that clearly helped my mind set up the idea of following the man in DC. And, last, I did have a long-ago ancestor who was a Baptist preacher, and his name was Prosper. I thought Prosper was too obvious for the poem, tempting as it was, so I changed the name and gave the line to a persona who was inspired by my wife—who actually was born in the Deep South.

Here is an example of a poem I wrote from my present, or recent past. From 2006 through to the present, my family's main vacation spot has been Old Orchard Beach, Maine. In this poem, I followed the setting rather than the personas, and the personas appeared late in the poem. In other words, I trusted that the freedom of the poem would find its way. The idea came from fact. Another way to put it is that I conceived and explored the meaning of the poem's title itself:

## *Old Orchard Beach, Maine*

Who would have thought a forest
Of ancient pine trees would grow
Half a mile from the beach,
Reaching so high that each needle
Slowly floats, like a tiny hang-glider
Turning and tumbling ever so gently
Before resting on a bed of sand
Covered in green and brown needles.

And who could have imagined a sandy beach
Right at the precipice of a thousand-acre
Apple orchard. The apples long gone—
Replaced by clapboard houses, pedestrians
In flip-flops, hands sticky with cotton candy
And salt water, salt air, hand-pulled salt taffy.

Once did pirates look through a spyglass
At green apples on green-leaved trees.
Now? Mothers look up at their children
High above, rocked to and fro, waving,
On an amusing three-dollar-a-ride pirate ship.

The Palace Playland with its Whac-A-Mole
And its nostalgic long-track ski-ball
Rests on a tract that was once a cemetery
Or perhaps the apple pickers' barracks.
Imagine those pickers now, rising up from
Their deathbeds, the lights and whirls
Of the arcade, the dollar changers, the pinball
And the noisy plastic bubble housing tiny plastic
Hockey players passing a tiny plastic puck
The size of a Granny Smith apple core.

There they are, still wearing their picker's bibs,
Their picker's overalls, the long day's work
Staining the blue denim in a sweet and sickly rot.
The cashier hands them each a quarter, to entice.
The bells and whistles beckon, a quick glance
At the ski-ball, the quarters quickly stowed,
Deep in pockets, each picker keeping a bony hand
Across the opening seam, protecting the day's pay.

---

As I was writing, the urge to populate the beach with people was strong, but my family did not fit, and I write from my life and my truth. So, when people finally entered the poem, it held that they would also, like the focus of the poem, be of the past. The poem was long enough and deep enough to handle a turn. All sonnets turn, and many free verse poems do as well. Simple words can do the trick. One of my favorite words (and you should contemplate yours) is *imagine*.

As you read the poem again, note the turn anchored and propelled by that one declarative word: imagine. I make no secret that my family poverty and the way it made me feel permeates much of my work. Why wouldn't it? If my will is to write from a place of truth, mine my past, and contemplate where I am now, how would this not permeate my work?

It is up to *you* how far *you* dig, what you expose, and whether it is safe and advisable to do so. That is entirely your choice. I am comfortable at my age, and where I am now, mining this part of my past, so I do. I rarely see a blank page. Some call this finding your subject or voice. I do not see it that way. I see it, simply, as mining your past. But be comfortable in doing so. It only works well on all fronts if you are comfortable.

Here is another head-on example of working with one of my subjects: poverty. Here, I use some indirection when I use the plastic bag as a concrete detail, rather than saying *poor*. It is ultimately a good enough poem, but because it is somewhat declarative of its subject, it ultimately is less successful. It is, however, a good example of using a title as the first word of your first line and of continued mining of the past:

---

## *Poverty*

It is a terrible thing, memory,
When it hits you in the shoe aisle
Of your local Macy's or Nordstrom's.
You are buying dress shoes for your son:

A high school choral concert, winter show.
You have placed six pairs of black shoes
On the bench, having not looked at prices.

Your son is shoe-horning his feet
Into one pair after the other,
And you can't get the image
Out of your mind.

Winter, you are eight years old.
Your mother ties a plastic shopping bag
Into a knot around your beaten shoe.
The bag is beige and smells of the oil can
It once held in the shed. The cashier is polite,

Compliments your son before placing
His new shoes in a free canvas bag. Your son swings
The bag as he walks through the garden of perfect
Mannequins—Izod golf shirts over pleated khaki pants.
Tennis rackets and mint julips in hand.

---

The details are plentiful, which begs the question: What is true and what is manipulated?

Well, for starters, we don't have those level of stores in my small town, but I have gone with my family, many times, to buy shoes. In reality, though, my family is very picky about shoes, and my wife tries to steer us to deals most times, but that is about it for what is manipulated in this poem.

What is true is that even though we had money for food and shelter, and even a car when I was young, my mother did not buy us boots. Feet grow. The notion of sneakers every year or two was all my family could handle. When it rained or snowed, our shoes got wet. No boots. At least not as I remember when I was ten or twelve years old.

The image in the poem about wrapping a plastic shopping bag around my shoes to get to school? True. Of course, I manipulated the bag. Rather than bombard the reader with the obvious teasing from schoolmates, I used the image of the oil can in a Dickensian manner to drive home the impoverished descriptor. That also allowed me a smooth contrast with my current *comparative* wealth, as I slid in the canvas bag in the next stanza.

The mannequins wearing Izod shirts is true, not just in the reality that such mannequins are in every store, but in the specific image of the Izods. This image came from my past, straight from the wealthy junior high school I attended through a quirk of zoning when we were forced to move from my grade-school house (thrown out by the wealthy homeowner so he could give the house to his son). The mannequins have tennis rackets in hand because I joined that fancy junior high tennis team, the only player on my team that had never had a tennis lesson. I had to buy Izods with my paper route money to fit in. And, just as a top-off, I had to buy my own sneakers because the Kmart shoes my mom bought us didn't exactly work for tennis in a wealthy junior high school.

The poem is a bittersweet reckoning of past and present. In many ways, this understanding that life is at once the present and the past is key. This is how your brain actually works: freely. Like free verse. Every decision you make is influenced by everything you have ever done or seen or heard or touched or thought. Keep working to bring everything together. It will come.

No matter what form your writing takes, it is important to stay honest to your worldview. Sometimes I write poems (and prose and songs) that are, of course, less *successful* than I want them to be, at times. But what I try not to do is to allow myself to produce work that is less *true*. The further I get away from my worldview, the more likely the work will be to ring false, and false work is always bad.

Your worldview is there, and if you can't put your finger on it, then simply write honest work, time after time, and in those pages *your worldview will emerge*. Your life made that worldview for you. No one else has that exact worldview. If you understand that, you will produce unique writing.

In its original form, in German, this word "worldview" is *weltanschauung*, and the translation, as I understand it, is "a comprehensive conception and apprehension of the world." I live by this word through my writing.

# — 9 —

# The Senses Matter More than Anything

## *But don't overuse them*

Every day of your life, you are interpreting the world through the senses that work for you. These abilities are met by the environment. The combination creates a continuum in your day that is so constant, it is easy to forget about it when you write.

And that is a mistake. Most of what you write should acknowledge the physical world. That physical world is a world of senses.

In terms of senses (assuming all are available), sight takes precedence in one's brain. After that, at least in our writing, poets tend to vary whether they rely more on sound, touch, smell, or taste. These are at least the senses we agree on.

If I have a poem that takes place in a natural setting, sight and sound are of great use. But often, the way a fruit tree or lilac bush smells may aid my poem. Perhaps someone in the poem eats a fruit from a tree or touches the ground. Of course, these senses tend to combine most of the time. Smell in particular cannot be overestimated in its powers, especially in its linkage to memory.

Here is a poem that uses the senses but does not overuse them:

## *Return of Lake Agassiz*

I returned with my wife to where the floods
of ninety-seven had wiped out the whole
of our neighborhood. Where all the houses
had peeled down like clapboard banyan trees,

and we stood in caked mud, careless children
wearing our Easter shoes an hour past church.
Our Siberian sniffed as we cruised the rubbled streets,
stood where kitchens had hummed with baking,

water-stained photographs blowing across
the un-mowed berms. Images of baptisms,
graduations, weddings, births. Divorced friends,
houses gone, marked by ribbons, nailed

into dying oaks, having barely survived
the return of the ancient lake, while the homes
they shaded revealed, imperfections. Our house
emptied of its contents, stiffly hoped to move

to a local museum, to die forever as an example
of early steel structure. My wife took one last tour
inside, and with a shale in her palm gouged its metal:
Do not tear this house down.

Often the key to sensory writing is to state something that allows one sense, and then move on in order to keep from getting bogged down into sensory overload—as a writer or reader. If I overload your senses, I risk you losing the narrative of the poem. In a way, that sense overload would be more of an exercise than a poem.

An example is when I mention the dog:

---

Our Siberian sniffed as we cruised the rubbled streets,
stood where kitchens had hummed with baking,
water-stained photographs blowing across

---

In this example, I move away from the dog's sense of smell, rather than linger. The reader links the dog's smell with the bakery, while understanding that the bakery smell is long gone. I also quickly move back into the sense most used, which is sight. In the case of "water-stained photographs," the use of the senses is actually not limited to sight, as the reader will likely imagine the way the photographs feel and/or the way it feels to walk along rubbled streets. Again, diction is the key. "Rubbled" means reduced to rubble. Rubbled, then, more easily means both "waste" and "rough fragments of stone, brick, or concrete, especially from debris."

It is impossible to not use the senses when reading this poem, but the narrative of the poem is never lost to the senses. The poem was written after walking these exact streets in Grand Forks, North Dakota. My wife and our dog, Aspen, were exploring the aftermath of the Red River flood, which happened the year before we moved to Grand Forks; the present and past mined together.

Here is another poem that utilizes the senses, this time a blend of tones serious and humorous:

---

## *Embarrassing*

What truer way to own embarrassment
Than to share it with the whole wide world.

In unrhymed couplets of varying feet
With no concern for terminal spondees?

Southern Louisiana, Charity Hospital,
Me sideways on the examination table.

The good Dr. has left the room, left me
All alone with my highly inflamed cyst

The size of a softball, the size of a Valencia
Orange, or a medium Vidalia onion. It smells

Like the onion, not the orange. The Dr.
Has escaped, not for air, or a smoke,

But to gather his council of wizards
Like my onion-cyst is a carnival, freak

Side-show, with yours truly along for the ride.
The council in white enter

In their jackass white ice-cream coats.
Two women, three men, one sporting

A large medical camera. My Dr. is smiling,
Clutching a grade school wooden ruler.

I clutch onto what is posing for my dignity,
A thin white hospital sheet.

It budges from its hospital corners,
Reluctantly covers my face, the onion blossoming

Outside the sheet. I am pleased to have
Avoided a flatulent Dutch Oven. I hear

The women discuss my onion: a possible
Case study. My Dr. taps his ruler against it,

Calls out a number in centimeters
That seems impossibly large. I envision myself

Famous, like Freud's *Wolf-Man*,
Before I hear a man in the hallway shout:

"Looks like MRSA to me." The jackasses
Stop giggling about my odoriferous onion.

Fingers reluctantly poke at me, at my hip,
My onion. Someone pulls at my sheet,

Asks, have I been spending much time
In hospitals. I remain motionless as the jackasses

Shuffle out, deflated. My Dr. un-sheaths
His scalpel; slices my onion through its bulb.

---

Once again, this poem began from a real experience. The writing of the poem brought about hyperbole, and the use of the senses drove home the reality of the poem's triggering event. I also find it easier to write humorously when the event is tinged with dark humor, as well as some intelligence. Without these anchors, it is easy to find yourself writing jokes rather than poems, which is rarely a good idea.

The great thing about writing through the senses is that it allows you to mine your very recent past. This next poem, in fact, was written just days after the actual event that inspired it. The senses experienced during the event were so recent, and also so profoundly marked in my brain, that I found it easy to gather them and build the poem. Again, don't make a list of senses or string them together. Instead, fit them into the narrative of the poem in an organic way. This grounding allows you to become more truthful with your exploration.

Here is the poem:

---

## *Dropping My Son at College*

Daytime. It was January, snow had fallen
the previous day. Now came winter winds
blowing easterly, trucks belting down Rt. 1,
their cabs giraffing over the swirl,
my son and I low-gliding in a Nissan,
gleaning spare glimpses of daylight,
obliquely forming between water molecules—
frozen, swirling, whipping, drifting—
bouncing as we drifted, hitting drifts
as we searched through the atmosphere
for the road we still believed existed.
Each corridor of blown snow worse than the last.
In between drifts, I ungripped the steering wheel
and together we ignored the noise—
skin ungluing from vinyl—
and I fiddled with the radio to calm
us. I attempted small talk
as if we were not driving a gauntlet,
as if we were not feeling like we had
simply gone too far to turn around. My son
beside me     his shape     still there
yet somehow ghostly—*as if he had himself*
*unglued,* first his hands, next his feet
from the rubber mat, my son lifted out obliquely,
searched for in the intermittent daylight.

---

Only the last four lines of this poem are untrue. Or are they? How do you capture that feeling of impending death without becoming philosophic? But the poem is grounded in sense details, and so I am afforded the luxury, the indulgence, of those last four lines of philosophy.

A little use here and there of italics, or space between words, or an em dash, are all things that can help break up the simplicity of your lines if used sparingly and organically. Again, as I will always point out to my students, place the lesser part of speech on your left margin (conjunction, preposition . . .) and be sure your last word is a *noun*, or occasionally a *verb*, almost without fail. Try, as well, to make a good portion of these last-of-the-line words *one-syllable words*.

Because I believe in the power of narrative, I do lean in that direction even when writing poetry. You could easily lean a bit more into the sense details; just be sure not to wallow. Don't show off; just get on with it. But always remember the poem is a whole, not parts glued together.

Here is an example of using the physical details of the world to explore the mental, emotional connection between two people. Notice that while we are not sure exactly what the persona is feeling about his loved one—perhaps recalling a car accident, or another time when things were different—we do feel the sadness. This occurs through the language itself, and that is in large part due to the focus on the physical world. Notice as well that sense detail is utilized, but not overused, to gain the realism of the moment.

---

## *Bathroom Phones*

I turn off my thousand-dollar cell phone
Clap twice to turn off my Tiffany lamp . . .
I have dreams and nightmares to witness . . .
But I am thinking about bathroom phones.

First time I saw one: in the Grand Hyatt Suite,
Twenty-eighth floor, Denver, Colorado.

Wearing my crisp white *Officer and a Gentleman*
Candy-assed room-service uniform. Brass

Buttoned, tight at the neck, I sat lightly
On the commode and dialed you at home.
You weren't home, of course I knew,
You had to drive from Thornton

To Ft. Collins, to submit a final term paper
In a blizzard. We were before cellphones,
A nostalgic time. Living in caves. I watched
Snow crystals freeze to the hotel windows

Up there in the clouds. The snow wreaking
Havoc below. I let the phone ring.
With my free hand I ran the hot water tap,
The warmth slipping through my fingers.

---

As you can see, every stanza has sense detail within it. Again, the sense most utilized is sight, but the sense of touch is the most important in the poem: that feeling of the warm water, and the double meaning of "slipping through my fingers."

# — 10 —

# Why Pentameters (Ten Syllable Lines) Exist

## *But does not need to be so formal*

Let us revisit my poem "Highway Blueberries." Notice that the first line, and many of the lines, do not end with a mark of punctuation. As I said, I want propulsion in this poem, and I also want to make use of my line length. Because my lines are long, I can use punctuation within them. Here is the poem again:

---

### *Highway Blueberries*

Logging trucks hug the first row, spewing thick black smoke
Carcinogens like atoms, a DNA double-helix of death.
The fog collects like trash on the roadside,
Before organizing in uniformed teams to descend
On this acre of high-bush Maine blueberries. Families
Have assembled in cohorts of threes and fours, the Amish
The Lutherans and the Atheists. Children play chess
On the human sized board, watching, and pointing,
At the smoke as it dissipates, fallout falling in between

Row after row of green and blue berries. New buds mingle
With full, berries straining to be reached in the thickness
Of untrimmed hedgerows. The smoke settles into physical
Soot atop straw hats and fingernails, the berries loose
In hands, filling bags and the footfall below. No one picks
The fat blue berries nearest the road. Another logger rolls by.

---

The first line works on its own, but it also flows into the second line. This enjambment is a hallmark of good poetry, as the emphasis on *line* that exists in poetry allows double readings. On one hand, we have the first line itself, which reads in an interesting manner. In addition, because the first line is still working in the second line, we have "smoke" connecting with "carcinogens" to create "smoke Carcinogens." The second line works even without the first, if fragmented, by reading "Carcinogens like atoms, a DNA double-helix of death." All of this comes from avoiding what I call left-to-right writing. If you write all of your lines as statements, left to right across the page, you lose the beauty of what I have just described: the way a line works off the preceding line or into the next line, forming connections beyond the line itself. The goal in poetry writing is to utilize tools, but sparingly, and only when they fit organically.

Another thing about line length of this ilk is that the lines are all *enough* words, especially if we use enough one- and two-syllable words, to create enough visual space and actual reading time such that we can lend added weight to the position of our final word. Again, each word at the end of your line, when possible, should be a noun. Occasionally a verb is necessary, and sometimes, for purposes of flow and propulsion, other parts of speech are the correct choice (such as my use of the word *there* near the end of the poem). But rarely is it effective to use anything besides a noun or verb in this final position.

This is not a theory. In practice, there is an elapsed half-second (or so) that occurs when we move from this last-position word of a line down to the start of the next line on the far-left side. Because of this slight reading delay, the final-position word is afforded a chance to *linger*. Again, *poetry is based on very small details*, and it is the understanding and use of these details that will raise the level of your poetry and its overall effectiveness.

Many young poets write constant short lines, even one-word lines, in an attempt to achieve this lingering effect. The problem with that approach is that too many short lines in a row become the norm, and thus the notion of a word standing out in relief disappears, as does all the possibility of enjambment. Furthermore, the poet does not hold our attention, demand our time, nor create space and detail for us to exist in. A few poets can and do pull this off, but, like painters learning line and light and shadow, the short-line poet has studied all of these parallel notions within the art form before taking to writing short lines. In addition, *I am convinced fear is at the heart of writing the short line in terms of the apprentice poet.* The belief is that less is actually exposed from the poet and so less is there to critique. The absence of all our poetic tools is actually glaring, and so in many ways, the poet has exposed fear and created more critique through absence. Fear should never be a default position in your writing.

The larger, simplest, and yet somehow difficult reason for pentameter is one I learned in my MFA program, and one I often share with my students. Many ignore it, often because the reality is that writing longer-line poetry is more difficult, with more juggled objects. *The problem is, the lesson can't be ignored.* Again, this is not theory, but fact. Here it is, offset and italicized on purpose so you can return to it again and again:

> *The English-language speaker, speaking in the usual breath, speaks eight to twelve syllables.*

In other words, the usual breath is three seconds, and the average English-language speaker will speak eight to twelve syllables' worth of words in those three seconds.

Poetry was originally memorized and spoken aloud. That is why pentameter exists, and why it matters. Pentameter means you use, generally, ten syllables per line. Variation exists, so the notion became eight to twelve syllables per line. If you read Shakespeare's sonnets, you will see the occasional variation above or below the number ten. It is not wrong to note that even in free verse, we do pay attention to some of the sonnet's principles, such as line lengths and the use of the turn.

And because a poem is emotive, and emotion has great variance, we realize that we might stray from the eight- to twelve-syllable notion in our work. Perhaps this line is nine syllables, and the next is six, and the next is twelve. Perhaps the whole free verse poem has variance like this. Add the number of lines, take the average, and see if you can at least keep the poem's average between eight to twelve syllables per line.

Look closely at "Highway Blueberries" and you will see that the poem works in part because of the line length. This poem averages thirteen syllables per line, pretty close to the eight-to-twelve notion. The reason I use this poem as an example is that it shows, for those who like to write longer-line poems, that you can pack so much in and yet essentially adhere to the eight-to-twelve average. If you are averaging many more (or less) than eight to twelve syllables per line, it is certainly worth considering a rethink and rewrite to tighten or lengthen some lines.

In truth, my poems average eight to twelve syllables most of the time. If you count and average "Poverty," "Old Orchard Beach, Maine," and "Three Rolls-Royces," you will see they all fit the eight-to-twelve notion. If you count "Fontanel," which is one of the shortest-line poems I have ever written, you will find that the poem averages seven syllables per line, even as it truly varies line length within the poem. It should be noted that "Fontanel" underwent significant rewriting to find those line lengths; reading the poem aloud again and again as I rewrote it is how I arrived at the final line lengths. So, even when I do not stay within eight to twelve syllables per line within a poem, I am at seven or thirteen. Non-adherence is baked into the notion of free verse, anyway. We are already rebelling.

# —11—

# Finding Your Voice

## *Why reading matters*

Read poems constantly with a notebook handy, and then put the poem you are reading away and write your own poem *the moment* a memory emerges.

In a way, that sentence could be this entire chapter. But I think it is important to address what it actually means when writers say you should steal from other writers. I once worked with a writer who said he means it when he says "steal," and that is advice you hear again and again. But obviously writers don't mean we should *copy*. If so, we would all have the same poem(s).

What writers mean is that even though only you know the people you know, have lived your life, see the world the way you see it, etc., *you actually don't have your voice yet.*

It sounds counterintuitive, but your voice is in the poetry already written. No architect designs a building without having studied the buildings that exist or have existed before. The way a poet finds their voice is by reading other voices.

In order to do this without stealing, I do exactly what it says above:

*Read poems constantly with a notebook handy, and then put the poem you are reading away and write your own poem the moment a memory emerges.*

Doing this allows me to gather both voices and ideas at the same time. I never pick the book back up as I write my poem, because—and here is the thing—I don't want to steal. I instead prefer the word—not "invoke"—but "evoke."

"Invoke" is direct and active. "*Evoke" is indirect and passive.*

"Evoke" means to draw out something latent.

Reading other poets evokes my memories.

If you can understand and adhere to the difference, you will never steal, but you will never face a blank computer screen.

It is important to note that it may take an entire book to find a poem that evokes a memory that actually becomes a good poem for you once written. And here's what might surprise you: that is a positive thing. How unselective and watered down would my work be if every poem I read reminded me of something that I actually wanted to write about, *and* I thought would make a good poem? *Watch out not for the poems coming too slowly, but the poems that come too fast.* Working poets do not create a *keeper* poem every day, so why should we expect to do so? It is part of the poet's job to not write, to have false starts, and in reality, to *read more than write.*

All this reading creates an envelopment of voice, which helps us to find and hone our own voice and cycles through every possible poem that may be lurking within us—if we read widely and often enough.

The key to reading for voice is to read many poems in a row by the same author and then read many poems in a row by a different author, preferably one with a very different voice than the previous poet. There are many places online, most especially www.poetryfoundation.org, to read the best poets for free. Local libraries have poetry collections. And while you should read some poets from days gone by, it is wise to do most of your reading in modern works. I try to read half of my poets from the twenty-first century and most of the rest from 1950-1999 with a few from each half-century prior. I have been fortunate to oversee my university's acquisition of poetry books, and I am thus very keen on variety. It also makes me realize the world is full of great poetry, and yet welcoming of more year after year.

An example of this in practice is when I once read a poem about eating in a restaurant. For whatever reason, the memory that came to my mind was of eating Saturday dinners with my paternal grandmother at restaurants. I immediately closed the book of poems—never got past reading that poem's first few lines, in fact—and never went back to reading that poem. The reading of several poems prior to that not only showed me the way that writer wrote, but also put me in mind of writing poetry. It is the same way anything works. Surrounding yourself with anything makes you learn what that thing is. Immersion is the word I prefer.

Here is the poem that came to me by simply reading poetry:

---

## *Red Lobster*

I am writing this poem at my desk
Under my Pinocchio lamp owned since
Childhood, trying to remember the name
Of the restaurant where we ate Saturdays
Twice a month to get my father's mother
Out of her house. I know my title is wrong,
A placeholder, for this was the 1970s,
And though I clearly remember Gifford's,
My mother would not allow my father's
Mother to follow us for Saturday dessert.

I can see Philly, my grandmother, clear
As I see my blue fountain pen, her hair
Tidied beneath a too-thin Russian scarf,
The kind she bought at Ben Franklin's.
Her off-white pearl necklace strung
Loosely around her neck, an occasional
Pearl cracked, its presence a reminder
To my mother that my father was too good

For a rural Marylander who pronounces
Washington with an R. The restaurant

Is visible even in the low light of my lamp.
Families like ours—women and men
With two kids and a widowed mother
In tow. A jukebox in the corner, scratchy
Records two years out of date, fake Tiffany
Lamps and a busy cigarette machine. A cup
Of broken crayons and too-cute children's
Placemats for the mothers to draw on,
Avoiding mother-in-law countenance.

The widows pick at their food, pick at
The children. (Lums. The name was Lums.)
My grandmother picking through her ancient
Coin purse, counting dimes like valuables.

---

It is also of note that this is a poem that begins by admitting the writing of the work itself: an ancient nod, one I most studied through metafiction, and one that has become more popular in the last few decades. Some consider this an acknowledgement that we are creating artifacts. *Notice that the word artifact begins with the word art and also contains the word fact (and I).*

Artifact is thus a good way to think of what you are doing when you mine your past.

In "Red Lobster" the persona is acknowledging the writing as if it is happening in real time through the discovery of the name Lums. These are techniques you can use, but again, it is a matter of being organic. The reason this happened in this poem is that I actually could not remember the restaurant name and so I chose a placeholder. Truth is, the name Lums came to me near the end of the poem, and thus, organically, the poem wrote itself.

Poets talk about the poem writing itself, or they talk about being a vessel. This is an example where that happened. The poem came to me easily, but only after much reading, and there was very little if any rewriting involved. Remember, this was not something I was thinking about and no amount of staring at a blank screen would have inspired this poem. Immersion within the language and syntax of poetry, the reading of poem after poem by a single poet's voice, then another poet; these are the bits of so-called magic that evoked the poem.

Your memory bank is truly a bank, and it is quite full and brimming. *The difficult part is not that you have nothing to write about, but that you have too many things to write about.* Reading allows your brain to make connections and immerse itself in poetics, and eventually, something singular rises to the top. It may be an image or a setting or a singular moment. Once that comes out, it tends to connect with other bits and pieces until it forms whole. Sometimes the forming occurs in the writing, and sometimes in the redrafting.

Because I was thinking of my grandmother, I was also thinking of my parents. The Pinocchio lamp came to mind for a simple reason. When I was young, that was my lamp. Sometime later in life, I saw it next to my mom's bed. Whether she used it to recall our childhood, or whether she needed a lamp and didn't want to buy one, I will never know. But the image of seeing it there after I assumed it was long gone struck me, and it made a lasting memory.

In this restaurant poem I used reality, or truths. Along with the manipulation of still owning the lamp, that was *actually* my grandmother's nickname (Philly) and Lums *actually* had those fake lamps I describe, and we did regularly get dessert at Gifford's ice cream parlor. My grandmother—my father's mother—was a widow and we did take her to Lums quite often. She always wore dime-store scarves and, oddly, wore an old, authentic pearl necklace.

By the time I wrote a couple of stanzas, filling the lines with details—facts from my memory—I had created a world that felt real to me and to my reader. At the end of that second long stanza, the subject of the poem revealed itself to me: my paternal grandmother's dislike of my mother. At that point, because I had a world of details, I was able to subtly discuss this dislike yet still continue to delineate the physical world.

Again, nothing matters except the details. The famous line from William Carlos Williams is always at the forefront of a poet's mind (and the minds of all writers, for that matter). Essentially, "Say it, no ideas but in things" means that you can't create worlds from abstractions.

I am a great fan of Newton's Third Law (for every action, there is an equal and opposite reaction), and so I do understand that absolutes are unhelpful. The lesson here is not that abstraction in poetry is bad; it is that abstraction works best when the reader is first grounded. If the poet allows you to exist in a real place in a real time with real objects and real people, the poet is then more able to spout philosophy, etc., and the reader more able to accept and appreciate such abstraction.

This all goes back once again to orienting the reader. If the reader feels oriented in a detailed world, then they are free to go somewhere else (i.e., to explore abstraction).

It should be said that although we sometimes *all* feel like we have *all* the answers, we know we do not. As you slip into philosophy and the like, you have to be wary. The mistake I most see is a slippage into platitudes. Platitudes are best left for kitchen signs. Instead, in a poem, try to work off the reality of that *specific* poem, using only the *specific* world that has been created.

As an example, in "Red Lobster" these are the final lines:

---

My grandmother picking through her ancient
Coin purse, counting dimes like valuables.

---

Notice that these lines stay with the poem. They are organic. When I am writing at my best, the final lines are there for me, naturally, at my fingertips. Rather than say, "Be mindful of the value in people, not things" or some such platitude, the lines are doing that work but at a deeper level, and remain organic to the poem itself. In addition, the reality of the grandmother's life is there, in those final two lines, for she went through her twenties during the Great Depression. In addition, an action is performed, which naturally keeps a platitude from occurring.

# — 12 —

# Poems for Fun

***In case writing isn't always fun for you***

I have found it worthwhile to write haiku and list poems (or whatever you want to call them) whenever I feel that the work of poetry has become too much work and not enough fun. This allows me to understand that at its core, writing is actually, or should be, a pleasure. This fun writing gives me a boost, which can also be gained by writing a humorous poem. Haiku seem easier to me than attempting a funny poem, and list poems allow me to cobble things together that are floating around but have not yet spawned full poems.

Here is a list poem:

---

## *Grocery List*

My bank teller paints all her nails chrome
Except the left ring finger she paints gold.

I once knew a woman with a bee-hive hairdo
Who thought rotary phones were haunted.

Three-handed pinochle uses a kitty.

I once read a poem where the poet
Referred to world news as gossip.

My wife and I love gossip so much
When bored we gossip about ourselves.

I leave my dog's paw hair wildly untrimmed,
Then tell her she looks unkempt and ugly.

When we were kids, we used to salt
Watermelon and red-ripe tomatoes.

In Louisiana my wife once argued with a Cajun
About the ingredients that make cous-cous.

If I were named America's Poet Laureate
Every poem would contain cous-cous.

I once believed the devil had a bad sunburn.

When I wake up every morning, my hair
Is perfectly in place.

My wife thinks I am an asshole
Because my hair is perfectly in place.

Milk, eggs, peanuts. Applesauce.

---

As you can see, I have played with the idea of a list poem and a grocery list and combined the two. In a sense, I have used this creative endeavor to create a poem that I find funny. Many of these statements in this list are true. I did believe the devil had a bad sunburn when I was a child. We did used to salt watermelon and tomatoes. My hair is oddly in place when I wake, and my wife does not think that is cool.

Like list poems, haiku can also be funny or serious, but the act of the five-seven-five syllable run is enjoyable. It can also be a good way to understand how to be efficient with syllables, as the more one-syllable words you use in a haiku, the more words and meanings you have to work with.

Here are a few haiku:

---

## *Teacake*

Is rich with berries
Vanilla or chocolate
Cake. Tea on the side.

## *Husky*

Pale blue eye, one brown
Each different than the other
Like David Bowie

## *Haiku 1*

In five syllables
I can say that I love you
Or tell you to go

## *PB&J*

Two bread slices first
The jam on one bread slice, nice
Peanut butter's last

---

As you can see, some of these are light and fun, and some are not. In "Teacake" I have used the title as the first word of the poem itself, and "Haiku 1" is part of a series I have worked on.

I like one-word titles in haiku, and that is one of my rules. You can make up your own, and haiku are malleable, especially if used as a writing exercise. Even a haiku can have depth, like I believe "Haiku 1" does, but again, be careful of sentiment and platitudes: they are a trap.

The key is to keep writing. I find that writing is a lot like staying in shape. Every day that goes by that I don't exercise not only makes it harder for me to stay in shape but also harder for me to start exercising anew. If I go a few weeks without lifting weights, I find it difficult to get back into it. When I do begin again, I badly pull muscles and also feel bad about my attempted and missed workouts. I get frustrated and then go for weeks or months without, all the while getting more and more away from what I had built. When I am in a good place mentally, like I am now, I can work out regularly for years without fail. Similarly, I have written regularly for years with no lost period of time. I am convinced the two successes are connected.

Like exercising, I try to write most every day. I have found that writing poetry (and song lyrics) is the easiest way to fulfill this commitment. Writing a single poem exercises my mind, keeps my writing sharp, and gives me a sense of accomplishment. More so, writing poetry and song lyrics keeps me in touch with my world in a way my normal daily thoughts do not.

If I feel like I am "written out," sometimes rather than write a poem, song, list, or haiku, I will simply read. I am seldom able to get through a book of poems without a poem sparking in me. Nothing suggests to me that reading and writing are linked more than this simple process.

# SONG

# — 13 —
# Writing Song Lyrics

## *A brief introduction*

Writing song lyrics is similar in many respects to writing poetry. It is the best place to scratch your rhyme itch and where so much rhyming work exists in our world. Writing rhyming form poetry (sonnets, etc.,) is best left for later, after you have mastered free verse. But, if you write song lyrics that rhyme, you will find it oddly easier to set rhyme aside when writing free verse. When you feel a rhyme coming on, write a song. When you are wanting to write poetry, read poetry and then write poetry.

And here is another thing: don't always listen to songs with words when you write song lyrics. If you do, you will find yourself thinking everything has already been written. The old phrase "paralysis by analysis" comes to mind. Instead, go to a quiet place or put on music without words.

Another method came to me by accident. It worked, and now I use it all the time. Play songs from another room so that you can sort of hear words being sung; catch some of the rhythm and some of the sounds of the words. You can almost make it out . . . you catch a few words . . . This allows you to spark. I put on wordy singer-songwriter stuff that does not overdo the chorus, songs I don't know every word to. Hard as that sounds, try to not use songs you know too well, or your mind will find the words of the songs too readily. New online technologies make this kind of listening far easier by automatically suggesting songs, singers, and bands you don't really know.

The great thing about writing song lyrics is that I find I can write a song any time I want, and I don't feel a pressure like I sometimes do in my poetry. It is a kind of off-day workout that keeps me limber—a yoga of sorts, a good stretching pose. I often am just noodling around but manage to write a good song lyric: one my sons' band then writes music to and sings. Sometimes they like the ones I like less. That is why output matters.

In fact, I have written so many song lyrics that when they rehearse a new one, I often ask them what it's called and then ask if I can see the lyric sheet. What is great about this is that once I turn my song over to someone else, it is theirs to manipulate. Again, I am not a musician, and many songwriters are not. The more I write, the less precious I feel about a song I have written. More are always being written. More work will come.

# — 14 —

# Song Lyrics are Simple

## *Or should be at first*

I do not mean to suggest here that writing lyrics is overly simple or that lyrics are simplistic.

But, if we recognize that most people are driven by melody and beat, etc., then it takes some of the pressure off. In other words, the simplest way to write lyrics is to write simply. This kind of writing also allows you to not get stuck in a holding pattern.

Practicing writing is like practicing anything: you want to do so consistently.

So, in this section, we will explore writing in an everyday fashion by writing simply, with an understanding that great songs are often comprised of simple lyrics. This may be the best way to start writing lyrics, and once you've had a chance to practice, then we can move on to utilizing some things we have previously explored. Let's start with this simple song:

---

### *Watch the Distant Sun*

Oh there ain't no way
To tell the troubles I've seen

You know like a pistol shot
Like a cold fire rings
Well if you could just see
Your way to me
All the way to me
Make it all right
Make it all right
Watch the distant sun
Watch the distant sun
Watch the distant sun
Watch the distant sun

Oh there ain't no way
To tell the troubles I've seen
You know like a pistol shot
Like a cold fire rings
Well if you could just see
Your way to me
All the way to me
Make it all right
Make it all right
Watch the distant sun
Watch the distant sun
Watch the distant sun
Watch the distant sun

---

Here is a simple song with nine actual lines and a firm use of repetition. Many of the songs you sing along to are, actually, quite repetitive. There is essentially one verse in my song. That verse uses a cliché in its first two lines and then upends a cliché in the next two lines. I write "rings" to connect with the "pistol shot" but attach "rings" to "like a cold fire." This creates a poetic nature; a bit off, a bit odd, and so the diction of "cold fire" is able to attach to "make it all right" and "watch the distant sun."

Now, the listener may not understand exactly what is going on here, but they will get a feeling that the human relationship being described is amiss, and yet can be fixed. There is a need—a human longing—and the person being sung to can satisfy that longing; and so right there, the listener is more than willing to sing that song.

It now needs only a singer to phrase the lines and provide angst, and a musician to write the music.

It can be difficult to understand how simple most songs are. If a good singer and a good musician have done their work well, you will be taken by the quality of the music and the singer's voice, and the song becomes a package. Thus, when you look at the lyrics, it is somehow too much to untangle. You can't *un-hear* the lyrics.

If, however, you look up some songs that you know are famous, but that you don't know very well, you'll soon happen upon one with simple lyrics that will show you, clearly, *just how simple the lyrics are*. By doing this, my lessons will become clear, and you will begin to see that simple lyrics are just as capable of becoming a great song as complex ones. The great thing is, anyone can write a simple lyric. After that, we can add some tools as we go along, and we can write more difficult lyrics.

Let's look at another simple set of lyrics:

---

## *YOU DON'T HAVE TO STAY*

You come around
You make me see you
You hang around
Like lightning strikes you
I don't have to stay
Don't come around
I have no time to play

Where would I be
If I hadn't met you
I would be free
If I hadn't met you

I don't have to see you
I can walk away
Don't have to see you
Go just walk away
Like some Svengali
Wish I never saw you
Wish I never knew you

Where would I be
If I hadn't met you
I would be free
If I hadn't met you

---

This is an example of simply taking an emotion, a feeling or statement in your head, and working off of it in a simple way.

The thought here is that of having met someone you *can't* seem to stay away from—a common problem faced in life, especially in youth. The lines are, essentially, all saying the same thing, yet somewhat differently. The repetitive nature not only drives home the desire to be *free* of the relationship, but also makes it clear through the repetition how much the singer *can't* seem to do so. Perhaps the singing of the song is the way to understand and accept the fate of leaving.

Here is a further example of writing (even more) to a mantra:

## *Believe*

Believe in yourself
Believe yourself in me
Believe in yourself
Believe yourself in me

Open the curtains
Draw back the shades
Leave the shutters open
Let cares fade away

Believe in yourself
Believe yourself in me
Believe in yourself
Believe yourself in me

Day follows the night
Night follows the day
The summer and the fall
The winter fades away

Believe in yourself
Believe yourself in me
Believe in yourself
Believe yourself in me

This song was performed beautifully by my youngest son, just him and his guitar. It is a mood song. Simple.

Here is another song that started with a mood and the age-old question of *what if*, which is a common theme in song exploration:

## *On the Radio Tonight*

Far beyond the ranches
Past these Texas fences
Sits the moon in the stars
Cradled there so far
Away from me
Away from me

I can hear the voices
In stereo tonight
Singing in harmony
Singing songs of you
Singing songs of me
On the radio tonight

On the radio tonight
Spinning some old record shining bright
From the local station through the satellite
Those songs of love and loss
In three-part harmony
In three-part harmony
Two lovers star-crossed
Were we truly sorry to see
Our future just pass away
Our love it was here to stay
Our love was here once to stay

I can hear the voices
In stereo tonight
Singing in harmony
Singing songs of you
Singing songs of me
On the radio tonight

If you were here
In these Texas fields tonight
Would it all be alright
Or would we long
For the love in the song
On the radio tonight?

I can hear the voices
In stereo tonight
Singing in harmony
Singing songs of you
Singing songs of me
On the radio tonight

---

That does not mean the mood in question must be sad or worrisome. A simple song can also be uplifting and beautiful:

---

## *When You See the Stars Shine*

If you wade out in the river
And if you pan all day for gold
I will wait endless days for you
And every night we will grow old

You with your gold-dust eyes
And me with my old love songs
We've passed this way before
This time we can't go wrong

When you see the stars shine
Wave your hands at me
When you see the stars shine
Never let me be

Come take this land come take my hand
Gaze to the far star-lights and see
There's no harm in life's happiness
Beyond the stars this galaxy

When you see the stars shine
Wave your hands at me
When you see the stars shine
Never let me be

---

There's a bit of wisdom and experience in the voice of this song, but the nature of the song is of beauty and hope. *Simple* can mean despair or happiness, or a mixture of the two.

Here is an example of mixing the two emotions, while keeping the lyrics simple:

---

## *I Forget*

I forget the love songs
I forget right and wrong
I forget everything
Except you, except you
I remember everything

I forget to go to work
I forget to stay home
I forget where I live
I forget everything
Except you, except you
I remember everything

I forget to lock the door
I forget to love you more
I forget everything

Except you, except you
I remember everything

Stay with me this time will be
Everything it never was
If you think you can forget about me
I think I can forget about you
Maybe together we can forget everything

I forget everything
Except you, except you
I remember everything
I forget everything
Except you, except you
I remember everything

---

Note that the last verse complicates the song. You could drop that verse, as a singer, if you wanted the song wholly positive. My oldest son often partially drops or repeats a line or re-arranges my lyrics.

None of these examples are hard to write. Find one line, a phrase, and write it down. Build around it. See if it works in repetition. Is it a chorus? Is it a narrative line that makes you think of an attaching line? Write down that line. Keep going even though it seems too simple. Find something simple and keep building.

That last example, entitled *I Forget*, came from simply thinking about how every day is about remembering things we have to do. That is where so much anxiety comes from. I began listing things after the phrase "I forget" and soon had a base of a song. Then I found the counterpoint: "not forgetting you." From that, I simply created a verse that dug in a little deeper, and the dichotomy became "if you think you can forget about me / I think I can forget about you." Point / Counterpoint. Idea / Exploration.

In "You Don't Have to Stay," I am essentially working the same way. Idea / Exploration. Point / Counterpoint.

Simple.

And again, write about what you think of. Because I have spent so much of my life in a vehicle, commuting or moving or traveling, I like all things road-related (I even taught a film class on road movies). Recently, I sat down and thought until I had a title and an opening line. Once you have that, the song will come.

Here is my most recent road song:

---

## *Just Another Rider*

Driving home from middle Tennessee
I heard a song reminded me of you
I pulled off at a truck stop to eat
That truck stop reminded me of when you
Were here were here were here with me

Driving this old broke Freightliner
Way out into the darkest of nights
Ten feet off of the ground the ground
No one would guess I don't like heights
I guess it's just another lonely night

Cause I am just another driver
On these dark and empty roads
I am just another rider
In this crazy one-lane show

But I think I see you sometimes
Sitting next to me in the ghostly night
Your face shining under the dim dash light
I think I feel you sometimes
By God that gives me a fright

Cause I am just another driver
On these dark and empty roads
I am just another rider
In this crazy one-lane show

Driving this old broke Freightliner
Way out into the darkest of nights
Way out into the darkest of nights
Way out into the darkest of nights
Way out into the darkest of nights

# —15—

# Using Your Emotions

## *And putting it all together*

In addition to rhyme and simplicity, song lyrics are also the place to utilize emotion that might lessen the quality of your poetry. In poetry, we want to talk a bit *around* our emotion—use indirection, all of our poetic tools—but in song lyrics, we often want to hit the emotion head-on, in part because we are aware the words will be paired with music.

I also think of a song as a moment when I express my emotional desires or describe a moment when I feel most vulnerable.

In a song lyric, I can say something more directly, even repetitively, whereas that might be too heavy-handed for a poem. Again, I know the music will help carry the art form.

Like poetry, the first line of a song matters. I usually sit outside or on a couch when I write, and if I just sit, a line will usually form. For instance, it was a sunny day on my back deck and music was playing in the house. I couldn't make out the words, but the rhythm and the tone put me in mind of the moment at hand. The sun was shining, a rare enough occurrence in northern Maine. No wind. Just warmth. In retrospect, this obviously brought to mind memories of my time in Denver. So, I wrote this line:

---

These days of lovely Denver sun

---

Okay, simple enough. I substituted Denver for Presque Isle. Note the way Denver gives me a rhythm. Specifically, the *n* in "Denver" works with my *n* in "sun," and the *d* in "days" with the *d* in "Denver." Simple use of sounds, yet effective.

Okay, now my mind is in Denver, where my wife and I lived when we were in graduate school and working forty-hour-a-week jobs. Our time off that overlapped was obviously paramount in its importance, and Denver was sunny and resplendent with outdoor activities. The first time we went to Denver, we spotted a snow-capped rocky mountain from the interstate as we drove in from the east. This was 1992, and it was spring. So, I easily found that in my memory, and the next lines came to be:

---

Where the Rocky Mountain snowcap
Is finally on its spring run

---

I was still sitting in northern Maine, so my mind found the next line:

---

Out in the woods run the maple taps

---

Are there maple taps in Colorado? I didn't look it up, I just kept going…and my mind was still remembering those three years in Colorado:

---

Take down the Mustang top

---

Okay, it wasn't a Mustang—it was a nondescript kind of ugly convertible—but I sat there and remembered renting it in the summer of '92, surprising my wife, and driving us to the top of Pike's Peak:

---

Let's rush let's have our fun
While we can still conceive it
Let's hush and watch the sun
While we can believe it
Drive up to the mountain tops
You in your skin and me in mine
Atop Pike's Peak where the Earth still shines

---

So, note that I am using some repetition of *s*, as well as *y* and *m*. Repeating letters or sounds helps the aural aspects of your poem if you don't overuse it. The idea of having fun "while we can conceive it . . . believe it" was obviously a reflective byproduct of living twenty-plus years in northern Maine, where I felt there was less to do than in sunny Denver, Colorado. "Skin" came from remembering that in Colorado, people showed skin in the spring, and in northern Maine's spring, not so much. Notice that one expects the cliché of "the sun still shines" but I have given it a new life by writing "Earth." And that came from being one with the earth, because that was Colorado in the 1990s. So, the Earth shines. . . .

Let's see the rest of the song:

---

One day we will remember
One cold day in mid-December
We'll sheer the wind enjoy this life
You know alright this life will stop
Look at me and you till we see the light
You know alright this life will stop
Look at me and you till we see the light
Till we see the light
Till we see the light
You know alright this life will stop
Look at me and you till we see the light
You know alright this life will stop
Look at me and you till we see the light

---

Okay, the last few lines drive home the song through repetition (and eventually the song repeats the line: "Till we see the light").

Prior to that repetition, the notion of memory appears but from the perspective of *then* imagining *now*. Northern Maine's long winters, here represented by December, time passing and eventual death (alluded to earlier by lines about believing / conceiving fun) . . . and the image of sheering the wind (driving a convertible) all explode together. *Till we see the light* hammers home the reality of life, time, and the notion of pursuing excitement in our numbered days.

The song is contemplative but simple. It was conceived simply by mining the past. When everything aligns, many songs are completed in one sitting, and they flow out easily once that first line is written. Other songs spring from a chorus, as lines are found to accentuate the ethos and pathos of that chorus.

Here is a chorus that came first, before the bulk of the song lyrics were written:

---

If your love is like diamonds you wait to sweep the dust
If your love-life is lying sunlight finds the rust
If you're leaving me now you'll hear my rebel yell
If this place is like heaven I don't want to see hell

---

Okay, so the second line came to me first:

---

If your love-life is lying sunlight finds the rust

---

And then the first line came and then the third and fourth. It was clear to me that the chorus should be as it appears above, so I switched the first two lines.

Each line is in the eight-to-twelve syllable range, more or less, so I wrote the lyrics to match. (Line length in terms of syllables is quite flexible when it comes to song lyrics.) Clearly, this was a song, an emerging song, of loss and pain. But I also knew I had the chorus down, and so in this particular song, why not have the chorus equal in time to the lyric? As I wrote, I wanted the chorus to echo and amplify and solidify what the lyric had to say. This is writing to the chorus, in my eyes, and it can be very effective. Here is the first lyric prior to the chorus:

---

Broke from our cages we followed the lines
Passed primrose paths got caught up on the vines
Counted ourselves lucky found out our beliefs
Passed all of the burned-out magicians and thieves

---

Well, my chorus speaks of the importance of diamonds and also of hell. These are both themes to which humans have attributed symbolism. This got me thinking about our animalistic nature, and so the word "cages" came to mind. The notion of an animal breaking out and finding its way through the woods behind my house in rural northern Maine gave me the vines; and "primrose path" had nice tie-in meanings. Now that the animal is me (or rather, us), the contemplation of beliefs returns, and the animal in motion passes what we all are at heart: magicians and thieves. And this is where rhyme in song helps. I needed a rhyme for beliefs.

Here is something important. Don't use your computer or a rhyming book. Not because it is too easy (though it is; more on that coming), but because it gives you weak writing. It creates *sameness*. Ever listen to a song the first time and guess some or most rhymes as they come? That literally happened this morning. I was listening to what I tell my kids is old-man Spotify (my cable radio station). My headphones are on and I am listening to a classic rock song I had never heard, and despite that, I manage to guess two-thirds of the coming rhymes. The weirdest thing is that in my mid-fifties, I thought I had heard every classic rock song. But, back to the too-easy part: I would never, in a book, have found *thieves* as a rhyme for *beliefs*. How did I do that? Simple. Try it. Go somewhere where no one can hear you and just start mumbling out words that rhyme with your original word. I do this alphabetically, which gives me the constant prep of a new letter. If I get to Zed and have no rhyme, I go through the alphabet again. Sometimes I start with an arbitrary letter and go backward. If I don't find a rhyming word I like, then I get out my pen and try that way. You will get some weird words, made-up words, everything you can imagine. And, again, try different numbers of syllables, and don't be afraid of partial rhyme . . . it works.

So, my lyrics are on their way, but the song has not yet built up to the chorus enough: my chorus would not fit after these last four lines, so I pressed on. Here is what I got next:

---

Driver said, "You can't leave after you enter this town"
We jumped from his pickup wind flowed through your gown
Settled for a trailer without youthful pride
Spent our lives spinning out thickened webs of lies

---

I had just passed burned-out magicians and thieves, so my still-in-motion animals/humans found their way into a vehicle, mostly because I wanted to keep up the "in-motion" idea. I often consider the fact that people tend to live where they are born, and because I've lived a bit of a nomadic life—from Virginia to Colorado, Louisiana, North Dakota, and Maine—I personally find that a foreign concept. At the same time, I did not leave Virginia until I was twenty-five, and before I left, I did feel I would never leave. So, here, I took the "can't never leave" approach. In other songs, I celebrate living forever in a small town. It depends on the song. The driver is a soothsayer or perhaps something else, and his tone is admonishing: "You can't leave after you enter this town."

Well, when you put it that way . . . so out we jump, and I do actually live in a town of pickup trucks, and if I throw in a gown, we get—and quickly—the image of newlyweds. The next line quickly places us as a couple, young and so poor, living in a trailer. The past is always there for a writer. I lived in a mobile home in college, and my neighbor's daughter once used our phone. She was talking to her boyfriend, and I imagined her here as I wrote—her and her boyfriend, and the way poverty repeats generationally. Now the song had reached a place where the chorus could come in. Here's that chorus again:

If your love is like diamonds you wait to sweep the dust
If your love-life is lying sunlight finds the rust
If you're leaving me now you'll hear my rebel yell
If this place is like heaven I don't want to see hell

See the word "rebel"? This trailer was in Virginia. I used to ride the Rebel Yell roller coaster at King's Dominion near Richmond, Virginia. That rhythm you feel reading the words comes from a simple idea as well: mining your past and considering sound, all the while making connections.

Use one-syllable words unless you need two. Notice in the chorus only a handful of two-syllable words, and none with three? Every word has meaning, so, the more words, the more meanings.

Okay, now my chorus fits my lyrics. Lyric of four lines, lyric of four lines, and then my four-line chorus. Now, I am ready for more lyrics. I have my characters (and they always start out as me / us and become someone else, or vice versa) in a fixed place now, and they're established as newlyweds with a rocky future. I reread my chorus. I want to repeat it after this next verse. What is in that chorus that I can amplify?

The answer is right there in black and white: *love-life lying.* I need that expanded upon in my verse. Here is the verse:

You worked at Jack's Diner some nights until three
Got friendly with all those magicians and thieves
This town's so small you see this end from the other
When you've made your way down no way to recover

Notice what I have done is organic. I have brought back the magicians and thieves. One of my characters has strayed from the relationship, and in a small town, that soon gets around.

Only after I am finished writing do I figure everything out, though the more I write the more I am somewhat aware of what is happening as I write; and the memory of the decisions I made while writing it forms and is remembered even now, years later. The impetus is, after all, within me/you. It is not magic. If you focus on what you are doing, memory not only opens up but works in the present as you write. I own my memories, and no one else has my exact memories. All I need to do is open up to them—and again, only if I am emotionally ready to do so. If I am not ready for a certain memory, I move on to one I can handle.

Did the diamonds in my chorus create the idea of the gown and thus the newlyweds? Likely. I also have a habit, as taught to me by several teachers, to look closely at what I have just written in order to see where I am going. Really, that's how all things in life are, aren't they? How often do we think about what we did today and what we should, therefore, do tomorrow? If I wrote those initial lines to start out, I want to trust them, because they are quite likely the most honest thing I will write in that song (or poem, etc.).

The chorus repeats twice. Here is the song in full:

---

## *Heaven & Hell*

Broke from our cages we followed the lines
Passed primrose paths got caught up on the vines
Counted ourselves lucky found out our beliefs
Passed all of the burned-out magicians and thieves

Driver said, "You can't leave after you enter this town"
We jumped from his pickup wind flowed through your gown

Settled for a trailer without youthful pride
Spent our lives spinning out thickened webs of lies

If your love is like diamonds you wait to sweep the dust
If your love-life is lying sunlight finds the rust
If you're leaving me now you'll hear my rebel yell
If this place is like heaven I don't want to see hell

You worked at Jack's Diner some nights until three
Got friendly with all those magicians and thieves
This town's so small you see this end from the other
When you've made your way down no way to recover

If your love is like diamonds you wait to sweep the dust
If your love-life is lying sunlight finds the rust
If you're leaving me now you'll hear my rebel yell
If this place is like heaven I don't want to see hell

If your love is like diamonds you wait to sweep the dust
If your love-life is lying sunlight finds the rust
If you're leaving me now you'll hear my rebel yell
If this place is like heaven I don't want to see hell

---

How do you decide on the title of a song? You choose something from within it, most of the time. Often you pick from the chorus, but as you can see here, that choice does not have to be an exact phrase. In the end, I felt this song was about that impetus of the final chorus line: *Heaven & Hell.*

Some songs are not short and simple. Sometimes a song comes and just keeps coming. When this happens—when you are not writing into a chorus and you feel the lines spilling out—do not censor yourself. Write what you are feeling . . . these are your songs, you know? That spilling-out feeling is a catharsis of sorts, and it is okay to feel angry or sad or to feel negative and positive at the same time in your art, if you feel you can handle the emotions. Don't censor yourself in your art unless you are unwilling to work with the emotion. I am willing to work with my love-hate relationship with places I have lived, so here is a long-lyric song that exemplifies all of this in its entirety:

---

## *Every Ghost*

Marriages sprung from junior proms and the devil's little tricks
Out past the burned-out Winn-Dixie they ride their Chevy sixes
You can't change the past or carry out your pageant crown
When the parade girls have packed it in when their dreams have all left town
Every ghost has come here for you and
Oh you hear them now
You hear them even now

You swore to your girl you'd take her to the world
Like your father told your mother and
Your girl swore to you my friend we'll make it to the end
Our lives will be like no others and
Every ghost has come and
Oh you hear them now and
In their Chevy sixes gonna get their fixes
Riding high for just awhile
On that rut-filled quarter mile
Their girls waving flags they smile
They'll be with you tonight
For just awhile
For just awhile every ghost has slipped away
The sun comes up and stays
For just awhile every ghost has slipped away

But time finds time to come around
Kicks you hard when you're feeling down
Your dreams were ruined in the backseat
The kids are coming fast
Your dreams are in the past and
Your love a ghost you swore you won't meet
You can see it in her eyes
You still see it in her eyes

This year could be the day
You might run away with your love and all your visions
Of a different life if you only might
Find a way out from under this derision
Maybe you are in the crypt
Your body has gone it's slipped
You feel the scars of your past thunder and
Out past the Winn-Dixie they still gather at night
Come together little devil gonna make it seem alright and
you know
Every ghost come from another
Like your father and your mother
You are every ghost born to another
Every ghost is just another
Every ghost is just another

---

I am not much of a musician. I can play a little of the drums. I can sing a little bit. I am a writer, so I naturally phrase my poems to read on a page. However, in this song, I tried to imagine it being sung, and so my rhythms were influenced by a little singing aloud as I wrote. In addition, I allowed the lines to follow my emotion. Reread them; do you feel the emotion? That is important, because whoever is singing these lines must emote.

My attraction to writing was initially fueled by the radio. I must have listened to more music than most kids on the planet. My parents' house was filled with record albums, some cassettes, a reel-to-reel player with rarities, and a constant stream of music. My father played records: 1950s rock (he was a part-time drummer and singer) and doo-wop and big band and California country-rock, while my mom was country to the bone. I listened to pop radio with my brother like it was necessary to sustain life. Later in life I took on several more genres.

What I learned as a listener was that every lyric could be changed, because someone had to make it up in the first place. By the time I had any ability, I would rewrite a rhyme or a phrase in a song as I listened and ask myself if mine was as good as the original. Even if it was, did it change the song in a way that added to or subtracted from the surrounding lyrics? That is what I remember when I write song lyrics. They are not meant to be precious. They should mean something to the writer, and then the singer. Lyrics should emote.

What if you just want to write a song full of clichés to go with cool music and forget all that?

Well, that works too. But when I do this, I still try to make it good by worrying about the diction and the rhythm and the rhyme and the line length and the progression of the story… all of that, even within a soup of clichés.

Want an example? Here is a song I wrote using only clichés, configuring it enough, but not too overly concerned:

---

## *Bet Your Bottom Dollar*

Well you can bet your bottom dollar
We'll try and make fine wine from water
Between the devil and the deep blue sea
This life is better than a kick in the teeth
They say beware of Greeks bearing gifts
They say Trojan Horses can cause rifts

Better the devil that you know
Than that old devil that you don't
Light a candle then curse the dark
They say beware the ides of March
The bigger they are the harder they fall
Cry havoc and buy something for a song
The dogs bark but the caravan rolls on
You don't change horses in mid-stream
Don't trust a lock if more than one key
Fiddling while Rome burns
You are flirting with disaster
Fiddling while Rome burns
You are flirting with disaster

---

I sneaked in some meaning in the last section. I used the beginning to push the song. But mostly I wrote the song as an exercise in writing to the coming music and to understand the nature, good and bad, of writing to clichés.

Here is another cliché song, but this time longer and with more attempt than the first to tell a full story using clichés. This is a good time to mention that the more you read, and the older you get, the more you will notice that in many genres most songs are entirely, or mostly, made up of a combination of clichés and known phrases. Because I like to write without clichés, for the most part, when I do write a song with clichés I tend to go all out. This method actually helps me remember not to use clichés when I write my usual songs, almost like I am emptying my head of clichés into a song, then I am able to write without them, or in combination.

Consider cliché song number two:

## *A Good Beginning (Bluegrass)*

You can't judge a book by its cover
You can't learn to swim without water
Now the bloom is off the rose
The frost is off of the pumpkin
You've gone off and you've chosen
To air dirty laundry in public

[Chorus]
A good beginning don't mean a good ending
The best laid plans of mice and men
Well now the boot is on the other foot
You were a day late and a dollar short
A day late a dollar short

I thought you were my diamond in the rough
Now I catch that falling knife you know it's right
You know it's death by a thousand cuts
Caught between Scylla and Charybdis
You've got champagne tastes on a beer budget

[music / tempo change]

I caught you with your hands in the till
Your hand in the cookie jar was filled
You can't have your cake and eat it too
You can't go where the green light leads you
God willing and the creek don't rise
You can't win for losing can't win for trying
You can't squeeze blood from a turnip
You can't teach an old dog new tricks

[Chorus]

A good beginning don't mean a good ending
The best laid plans of mice and men
Well now the boot is on the other foot
You were a day late and a dollar short
A day late a dollar short

Blunt words have the sharpest edge
We all know Daniel came to judgement
So don't get your nose out of joint
If your foresight was as good as your hindsight
We would be better by a far sight
Now my new gal's bright as a button
She's shiny as an unspent penny

I'm caught between the devil and the deep blue sea

[music / tempo change]

This life without you ain't what it's cracked up to be
She ain't you though and
I ain't your new beau
Maybe someday I will give you a ring
Maybe I should've given you my ring

[Chorus]
A good beginning don't mean a good ending
The best laid plans of mice and men
Well now the boot is on the other foot
You were a day late and a dollar short
A day late a dollar short

---

In "A Good Beginning" I have also written in where I felt the music or tempo should change. You can do this and then erase them, or leave them, or not think about them to begin with. Again, I believe it helps me. If you are a musician, you will naturally either already have music, or you will likely use your guitar or piano as you write lyrics, and you will create tempo and rhythm as one.

Notice I have used some well-known phrases but also some clichés that have faded with time in such a way that they become, depending on the listener, not clichés. I know they are clichés, and, again, that is what is important. As the writer, I must be in charge of when and why I use clichés. And yes, the obvious title for this song is "A Day Late and a Dollar Short." Here is a case where I have also used a parenthetical title. So, the actual title is, "A Good Beginning (A Day Late and a Dollar Short)."

If you ever wondered why such parenthetical titles exist, that is why. I know the obvious title, and thus the parentheses. The true title was written from the chorus, as it speaks on a macro level about relationships—the way we start out being so different from the way we end up.

You can see this in the song's opening. If you are like me, a writer but not a musician, you do not know how the musician will interpret your lyrics. At first, this may seem daunting: after all, as the writer, you created the song. However, it is good to remember that as a writer, you are only in charge of the words. Here is a song I imagined, at least as I began to write it, as a psychedelic 1960s tune:

---

## *County Fair*

Licorice and morning dew drops, summer rain and lollipops
The breezy honeysuckle, Southern comfort home ramshackle
Grandma's porch white rockin' chairs
Mississippi delta is callin' me, callin' me
Out past the cypress at the county fair
You and me and sister golden hair
Day turns to night we didn't care
Out past the cypress at the county fair
Cousins playing banjo in the summer breeze

Fireflies lighting in the distant trees
Farms all tended the tractors out of sight
Gather 'round family singing through the night
Out past the cypress at the county fair
You and me and sister golden hair
Day turns to night we didn't care
Out past the cypress at the county fair
We while our lives away family as thick as thieves
Making jug-band music singing of love and peace
Smile as you sing your songs of grief
Dogs at your feet loyal with their sleep
All the way through the moonlit night
All the way through the moonlit night
All the way through the moonlit night

---

Now, to be fair, the lyrics seem to abandon the psychedelic ideology pretty quickly and retreat back to a folk / rock / Americana song (which is where my sons' band naturally sits). The point is, it turned out to be a folk song with an odd opening line, but it took hearing it with music to see what I had done in the song (however obvious it looks to me now).

But where did these lines come from? Well, I grew up in Virginia, where fireflies were how we saw our way at night. My father sometimes took me to see bluegrass music played, hence the banjo reference, an instrument my youngest son now plays. My favorite Christmas video when I was young was about otters playing in a jug band. We went to Florida when I was young, and I was fascinated by the cypress that grew in the watershed. We were out all day, as it turned to night, playing with cousins/friends and watching fireflies and listening to music. Honeysuckle aroma was omnipresent. My mother loved to eat licorice. . . .

So, even though I have been to my share of county fairs, the song is really, if indirectly, a meditation on my childhood. As the images flooded my mind, I wrote them, but manipulated my past just a bit into that desire

I have always had about living a more bluegrass life than I ultimately did. That came from being free and open as the song came: relaxed.

Sometimes, though, you just want a true country song, and here is such a straightforward, write-it-as-it-comes, simple country song:

---

## *Gonna Find a Way*

Well I'm sitting here baking in the sun
Gonna try to do it all over again
From the start, yeah, from the start
They say the past makes your future change
They say a man can find a way to re-arrange
The shadows hanging on the wall

Something finds you something shines a light
All the time when you're hiding in the night
Gonna find a way gonna make it alright
Tonight, oh tonight, on and on tonight

Okay so you grew up and got away
Found a new town gonna make a new day
A girl by your side a dog trailing behind
You buy an ice cream cone and watch it melt
Inside a little wedding chapel you say
I do you say but it fades away

So no one asks to hear a sad song
And no one asks to be strung along
But sometimes it's all that you can do
Just to hang on and wait for a brand new day
Put on a new record under the moonlight
You know there's got to be a better way

Something finds you something shines a light

All the time when you're hiding in the night
Gonna find a way gonna make it alright
Tonight, oh tonight, on and on tonight

---

Just like reading poetry to find your poems, listening to various music genres over the years will help you find your songs. If you have listened to hundreds of country songs (or perhaps thousands?), then just sit down and write. Put yourself in that place where you listen to what is in your head, those fragments of memory about what country feels like. Don't play any country music; just feel the country music. If it is already in you, it will come out. Trust yourself. Write a line that describes the here and now: "Well I'm sitting here baking in the sun" was my reality. Then I moved into loss. Remember, things are working out or they are not. It's usually that simple. I chose not working out but tinged it with hope. As I was writing, I remembered eating ice cream cones with my wife on our honeymoon and stopping to pet a dog, so I put that in the song. If you are thinking of something, well then you must think it fits somehow, or you wouldn't be thinking it right then. Write it down. You can move it or cut it or expand it later. Write it down.

But what about pop songs, or rock songs? How can you use all these tools to make one? Again, your musician will ultimately decide (if that is not you) which genre the song is. I have taken that to heart over the years and have tried to write songs that are malleable. Here is a song that can be performed as either pop or rock:

---

## *SPEAK OF LOVE AND LOSS*

You cross the room
Like your hair's on fire
You worship the moon

Like your heart's on fire
You wear a blue dress
Ladies breath in your hair
You enter a room
Like your God's caress

[Chorus]
You speak of love and loss
You really just don't care
Speak of love and loss
Like you just don't care

You make your way
Living on your charms
You know baby some days
Love falls from your arms
And you find yourself
Alone in a mirror
Your tangled youth your pride
It's all no longer here

[Chorus]
You speak of love and loss
You really just don't care
Speak of love and loss
Like you just don't care

---

Once again, these lyrics came from a first line. Doing nothing, not trying to write, the line "You cross the room like your hair's on fire" came to me, so I wrote it down. When I composed the song, I split the line to get a shorter, more pop-rock line than I often want in my folk/Americana lyrics. "Hair on fire" made me think of another well-known phrase, "heart's on fire," and so I wrote the lines that begin the song. If you like certain things, put them in your songs. I like the moon, and my favorite color is blue, and

I always thought lady's breath was a weird name for a flower worn in hair. In they went. I am fascinated by charm and grace and pride and, of course, loss. I managed to fit most of these thoughts in here.

What you begin to see is that these are not just words thrown on a page. These songs you write are a glimpse, sometimes a full stare, into who you are as a person and how you view the world. That doesn't mean everything you write is true. Much writing starts in truth and is manipulated. The world around you only looks the way it does and feels the way it does to you. Only you have that exact worldview. It is not right or wrong, but it is *your* worldview.

Here is a song that exemplifies everything we have explored. I imagined this song in an Americana style, named it that, and so I wrote in ideas for the music along with the words:

---

## *Americana*

In our small town flags line the streets
The young kids laugh, sing through reeds
Loggers roll by on rutted streets
Big and wide as the $4^{th}$ of July
The sky above blue and open
Out on the farms the prayers bring hopin'

[Chorus with steel guitar]:

Americana, American [last syllable of "American" rhyming with "Tron"]
Americana, American

In our small town we've served our country
In our small town time stands still
If you venture off your front porch
You will find all our streets are filled

Big and wide as the 4th of July
The sky above blue and open

[Chorus with steel guitar]:

Americana, American
Americana, American

In our small town we've ridden fences
Made our wares and done our mendin'
Some folks stay here and some folks go
Take to travlin' with the medcin' show [misspellings create the syllabic tempo]
Those who stay we bury with kin
Those who stay live without sin

[Chorus with steel guitar]:

Americana, American
Americana, American

If you venture off your front porch
You will find all our streets are filled
Big and wide as the 4th of July
The sky above [pause] blue and open
Americana, American
Americana, American

---

Notice that the last verse is repeated, but truncated for effect. The chorus is short, like a mantra. Its repetition drives home the song. Again, never forget the usefulness of repetition in song. Not every song has or needs repetition, but it can often make or break a particular song.

My town has logging ruts in the road. The "Fourth of July" section is abstract, but it came from my town's love of shutting down Main Street for city block parties. The parades are a big deal. All of that makes this town different from the big cities I have lived in. The notion of whether or not it is okay to leave my small town is an argument, one I have heard from many folks. We have farms and prayers, and small towns like this see their fair share of military service. That is all in my present, manipulated a bit in lines like "the kids singing through reeds."

Now, let's look at another chorus-comes-first song. I find my sons' band (technically they are a duo) enjoys performing songs with a strong chorus, one they can center the music around and repeat and move about and so on. This chorus is an example of how you can use a chorus to show off your poetic ability a bit. Here is the chorus:

---

[Chorus]
I want to shine like the moon in its crescent
I want to find harmony and luminescence
I want to hear you speaking in tongues
I want to remember you were gone all along

---

See how the chorus is kind of like a tight, short little poem? You can feel that it already has a rhythm. As we have explored before, a rhyme can be more than one-syllable simplicity on the page, yet still sound quite simple when sung. Here, I have used a very long word in "luminescence"—four syllables in fact. Notice that the lines are (even though one has a four-syllable word and another no word beyond two syllables) all in that eight-to-twelve syllable range. So, I had room for a three- and four-syllable word in one of the lines. Three of these four lines are ten-plus syllables. Longer lines like this afford room for more things you can try. "Crescent" / "luminescence" is a rhyme I am proud of, and my musicians appreciated it. "Tongues" / "along" works well, and feeds off repeated *o* and *g* sounds. . . .

Okay, what about writing even longer lines? It can be a lot for your singer to find their phrasings, but sometimes long lines create opportunities for your singer. Long lines usually mean longer songs, and that provides opportunity for your musicians to try new things as well.

Here is a long-lined song:

---

## *Resurrection*

Have your fun 'fore the sun wears you down leads you along
Downtown on roller skates the freaks are singing their songs
The muscle-heads doo-wop singers on old cornerstones
Dance with the swingers your loans you can't pay or face all alone
Beating out time at the five and dime singers awake and on fire
No chance at life for miles cars and bricks playing pickup-sticks
Carjacking for fun on the weekends shoot the shit over blue ice
Charms and stolen bracelets dangle from your pale wrists

[Chorus]
There's a resurrection tonight in old Hollywood
Find your direction strike a match set your spark tonight
In old Hollywood
This town is meant to leave your mark in old Hollywood
Oh mymymymymymy

Windows stare you down merchandise to wear
You fear you will never ever get there
So you take the next flight out of LA-X
Wind up back home on a light-sabre jet
Start again in the morning find your way down the line
This city is a ride through bone-dead streets of bone-dead-crime
Up above is like dust at your feet is the sweep
Of bright lights and city jewels no one seems to keep

[Chorus]
There's a resurrection tonight in old Hollywood
Find your direction strike a match set your spark tonight
In old Hollywood

This town is meant to leave your mark in old Hollywood
Oh mymymymymymy

Pitch your tent with the cold-wet homeless tonight
Settle in take a film home with you tonight
Sand and time are up to their old tricks
Gather round sing and dance through the night
Waves crash the shore in defense of you tonight
Clouds roll by they don't seem to stay make your way
Through the circus there's no admission today

[Chorus]
There's a resurrection tonight in old Hollywood
Find your direction strike a match set your spark tonight
In old Hollywood
This town is meant to leave your mark in old Hollywood
Oh mymymymymymy

Plant a garden plant your feet, dig in and feel the light
The old town streets of New Mexico tonight
Cobble stones three hundred years old
Misappropriation does not make it right
Just enough to get you through winter
Just alive and keeping cold
Basket weaving in the streets rice at home in a bowl
Baked in the sun like red clay in deserts undisturbed
Out of sight in a siesta of friends old and new
Sky is red sky is green sky is never blue
Farms dry as kites high in the summer sky
On a string children sing and cry with all their might
Calloused hands on the women their men have all died
They cried and cried until Jesus took their sight

[Chorus]
There's a resurrection tonight in old Hollywood
Find your direction strike a match set your spark tonight
In old Hollywood

This town is meant to leave your mark in old Hollywood
Oh mymymymymymy

---

Where did that all come from? Again, mine your past. Remember everything all at once and write...

There's that five-and-dime again, a part of the 1970s for me just as the roller-skaters were; the sun, another favorite; and a not-so-favorite part of my memory: crime. I lived in the Washington, DC suburb of Arlington, Virginia, from 1967 to 1985, before moving westward to other suburbs. In the years of my coming of age, DC was crime-ridden; at times, Louisiana was too, when I lived there. Crime, a somewhat prominent feature in my work, rears its ugly head. And when you are writing long lines—fourteen, fifteen, sixteen syllables and so on—you can really mix in so many things. That is the important word: things. That old chestnut of *only things matter* is true for a song like this. Populate your work with things . . . and people. Like this line:

---

The muscle-heads doo-wop singers on old cornerstones

---

There is my dad's doo-wop, and my college fascination with all things muscle (Arnold was big in the 1980s). Note that the song has speed, in part because I am declaring what you (the listener) should do. I am not really talking to the listener, of course; I am having a one-way conversation with the ether, but more likely with myself.

Again, pepper in *known phrases* to help people sing your song (they love how easily the words stay with them, even if they are unsure how or why that is happening).

This verse is a good example of mixed-in clichés:

---

Pitch your tent with the cold-wet homeless tonight
Settle in take a film home with you tonight
Sand and time are up to their old tricks
Gather round sing and dance through the night
Waves crash the shore in defense of you tonight
Clouds roll by they don't seem to stay make your way
Through the circus there's no admission today

---

You notice them more easily now . . . "Pitch your tent" and "up to their old tricks" and so on. . . .

But that is a lot of long lyrics, so in this case, it can be wise to simplify the chorus. The chorus here is really quite simple and open to the singer's whims as to how it can be done; a break from the demanding lyric phrasing:

---

[Chorus]
There's a resurrection tonight in old Hollywood
Find your direction strike a match set your spark tonight
In old Hollywood
This town is meant to leave your mark in old Hollywood
Oh mymymymymymy

---

As off-tangent as the lyrics seem to get with my memories and my *of-the-moment words* finding their way in, the song keeps working with the title, chorus, and overall main idea of old Hollywood. It does not take much to keep a song grounded, and I find that knowing the chorus or a title going in (in other words, writing to the title) can provide this grounding.

But the chorus is, after all, what most listeners attach to, unless the song is one that tells a story. Here is another example of a chorus from which I attached lyrics:

---

I've seen it all now I've seen enough
This world is hard this world is rough
If you've got the time please save my soul
Take me in part or take me whole

---

For this chorus, I made sure to write it in a way that sounded like it was to be sung rather than read. This is a constant bit of cerebral work when you are writing songs versus poems, and it goes both ways, meaning that if you primarily write songs, you have to remember that, in contemporary works, most poems are meant to be read and not sung. This sounds easy enough, but it's something I often see young poets struggle with, primarily because they hear thousands of songs a year but rarely read poetry. The only way to fix that is to read poetry constantly before writing it. But when writing song lyrics, you have more freedom.

Sometimes your lyrics are simply not as good as your chorus. It happens. Here is the song in full, and in my opinion, my chorus is better than the lyrics, which is often easier to get away with than a weak chorus and better lyrics (unless, again, your song is telling a story):

---

## *Siren's Call*

We were young and we knew it all
We listened for the Siren's call
Stayed out all day 'till the dinner bell
Threw Lincoln pennies in the wishing well

They say out of sight means out of mind
Still walk the tracks on the county line
See where we've been see we've done our time
They say you never leave the stars behind

I've seen it all now I've seen enough
This world is hard this world is rough
If you've got the time please save my soul
Take me in part or take me whole

This old world has changed I do say so
I've packed my things now it's time to go
We were young and we knew it all
We still listen for the Siren's call

I've seen it all now I've seen enough
This world is hard this world is rough
If you've got the time please save my soul
Take me in part or take me whole

---

Of note in this song is a tool I like to employ, which is to reuse part of a verse in another verse. You can see that I have wedged this bit between the twice-repeated chorus. Needless to say, when my sons' band plays this song, what sticks out is the chorus, and that little bit near the end helps.

Now let us take on the writing of a story song. Say you are staring at a blank computer screen. Like in fiction, a story song is usually set quite strongly in a particular place. If you conceive the setting first, it is like backgrounding a canvas. I am sitting outside right now on a warm and oddly sunny spring day in northern Maine. I am thinking that my wife mentioned that we need to uncover the succulents out front; do some weeding and such. Today would be a good day for that, and perhaps I will do it later.

I rarely write about where I currently live, though, as I have now lived in Maine for twenty years, I do so more than I used to. Living elsewhere forces you to write from memory (which is lovely because what comes to mind is inherently from truth, yet through the filter of memory, is also inherently false) rather than the actual inescapable facts staring you in the face. Maine is right there in front of me, but other places I have lived, and even places I have visited—those places allow me to draw on those lovely false memories. Memory allows for easy manipulation, as I know I have already manipulated everything through my own impressions, and, of course, the passage of time.

The succulents in the front garden have reminded me of the time my wife and I drove from Colorado to visit Arizona and New Mexico. This would have been in the early 1990s, and I have built up a certain nostalgia around that trip. It doesn't have to be like that. I could easily think back to our last family vacation in Old Orchard Beach, Maine. But the succulents, and our indoor cactus collection, those came from having lived in the West. And so, my thoughts of weeding the succulents in the front garden have attached to my memories of the West.

In order to write a story song (which I am honestly attempting to conceive right now as I write), I am going to choose that 1990s trip to Arizona and New Mexico. Next, I need to find my characters and my story. I like to conceive of these together, as images tend to come to me of both in tandem. I am also still aware of my setting. Right now, my setting is quite macro. As micro images come to me, I jot them down:

A native woman selling tourist trinkets along the market avenue in Albuquerque has always stayed with me. In Arizona, there was a Tex-Mex restaurant as good as any I have ever eaten in. Another al fresco restaurant in downtown Phoenix. The clean streets of downtown Phoenix. The valet speeding off in my wife's little coupe car. The Phoenix Zoo. The band we saw in Albuquerque that stood with their backs to the audience, behind a curtain. The array of pubs nearby, lined up in a crawl. The way the warm, almost sultry, yet cool-at-night air felt in early- to mid-March, having come from the lingering cold of Colorado. The way we could walk to almost everything from our wealthy Phoenix and Albuquerque hotels. The barrio so near the pub crawl, and the way the two worlds bumped up against one another. The joy in the children as they screamed and played in the school playground, somehow oblivious to the connective/divider between the two worlds.

I come back to my memories list and note there is a lot about food and drink. Very domestic. So, naturally, I follow that lead still thinking of characters and story. My wife and I were so young; not yet married. So, I try manipulating these facts. What if we were already older, and what if we were already married? What if the trip was not happy, as I remember it, but instead sad? What if, in other words, this trip was not part of a beginning but part of an ending? What if these backdrops of food and music and long walks were not peaceful, but instead intense?

I have, now, my story and my characters. My couple is fortyish (not twentyish), falling out of love (not deeper into love), married, and this trip is about uncoupling (not coupling). My wife and I have kids, so I imagine this couple with none. My wife and I have good jobs, so I imagine this couple with less.

My couple has no children and are poor, and on the verge of divorce. Perhaps they took this trip as a last chance to save their relationship? Maybe this is where they honeymooned, having taken a bus or borrowed an old car to get there, maybe from southern Colorado in a small town. Pueblo always drew me, because when I was a kid there was an ad on TV and the place you would write to for government information was Pueblo.

My couple is from Pueblo, which would have been quite a bit smaller when they were young. They are eating at the sites where they ate in Arizona and New Mexico, but all the places have changed. This is a key element in my life because each time I visit a place I used to live, I scarcely recognize it. This actually helps my writing, because it forces my memories to become more vivid, and more important, and that helps me write from them.

My couple is poor but has pride. Just like my family did. In fact, because my parents had good credit and used it, sometimes it was hard to understand our poverty. My couple is not angry at one another. Now I want to think of framing this, particularly by considering point of view. I want to mention what they dreamed when they were young. So, I choose teacher as the profession, maybe because I am one or maybe because of the barrio school I just mentioned, wherein they might walk and remember.

From my yard right now I hear a motorcycle, too loud and show-offy for my tastes, but it puts me in mind of the noise I had forgotten, and still forget, when I remember New Mexico, which is beginning to win in my head as the setting. I contemplate whether their world will be immersed in the world of New Mexico (traffic; other people around them; interactions), or if they will exist in a dreamlike world of memory, wherein things like a blow-hard motorcyclist do not exist.

Because I may not be in charge of the melody the singer ultimately picks, I do write with a melody or rhythm, and that melody is in my head, and that is how I find lines. When I am ready, I can follow this idea for a story song. If I do, I am sure I will write the chorus first, one that will repeat an idea or message that enlivens the song each time it is sung.

The last songwriting discussion I wish to cover is one of *favorites*. What kind of songs are you most prone to attach to from the very beginning? For instance, I listen to and like so many varieties of music, so many song genres, but the one I'm most attached to—the songs I played on jukeboxes in the 1970s and on my belt-drive turntable at home—the kind I memorized and sang and was moved by, as a writer and as a listener—was the ballad.

Whether it was folk music or country or California country, or pop, or rock, and later on, the metal power-ballad, it was always that bitter-sweet style that called to me: the ballad. So, if you're attached to a particular type of song, you should definitely attempt to write one in that style. Not only do you have an interest, but you have a kind of muscle memory built up because you have heard so many songs in that style or genre.

My grandfathers, unfortunately and sadly, both died somewhat young. My father's father died before I was born, and my mother's father died when I was very young. That always left me thinking about how my grandparents were denied the grace of growing old together. My own father died in his fifties, as both my grandfathers did. My mother too, was sadly denied growing old with my father.

Because I am always thinking of writing from what is real, writing from my past and a place of truth, and then manipulating, the song "One More Walk" came to be. It is a tearjerker, and I remember my wife crying when she read it. My being an artist, her tears were all I needed to know about the song: it worked. My oldest son has taken a crack at it, but it is so emotionally weighted he has never pursued it further. It is an obvious piano ballad. Here it is:

---

## *One More Walk*

When I was a boy no more than seven
My grandfather made his way to heaven
And before he passed away
I heard my grandmother say

Can I take one more walk with you?
Can I have one more talk with you?
Before your time with me is done
Before your life with me is through

Down in Virginia down at school
Where they all teach the golden rule
I found the devil has his way
Before he went I heard father say

Can I take one more walk with you?
Can I have one more talk with you?
Before your time with me is done
Before your life with me is through

Now I have grown into a man
I know Lord above has his plan
Love when that time comes 'round our way
Will we both smile and then say

Can I take one more walk with you?
Can I have one more talk with you?
Before your time with me is done
Before your life with me is through

---

My grandparents were Catholic, and so that truth is written across my lineage. My parents were also raised Catholic, and so in the song I simply honored that lineage. Simply put: Write from a place of truth, remember what you remember, how you remember it, and manipulate as needed to fit the work. The work truly is the boss. When I am writing, I am working. And so are you.

For what it is worth, a note on workspace: Where you are able to work your best is where you should work. The notion that a writer must have a nice desk and a certain pen only works if that is what the writer thinks they need.

I have written with anything I have. I have used a crayon on a tissue. Seriously.

The computer is perhaps best for poetry and song, as it is tidy and thus allows multiple drafts that you can keep and easily compare. If I am writing a longer work, I prefer handwriting with a decent pen on a yellow legal pad. You will have your own preferences.

In what place, and when you write, and with what, is often dictated by your life. The important thing is that the work gets done. If your phone works for you as a writer, use it. If you want to carry a tiny notebook and use that, go for it. The work matters; the rest is pretense.

And last, I will say, write with a clear head. Be sure you want to explore what you are exploring, and if so, use your intellect and emotion in tandem.

# — 16 —

# How to Revise Fiction, Poetry, and Song

## *And not fake it*

You must find a revision method wherein you actually revise. If you try a method and find you are doing very little in terms of actually revising, then that method is not working.

It is that simple.

Revising means finding and highlighting what works, then finding and correcting (or removing) what does not work.

It is that simple.

What this means is that you either have to find a workshop group you trust, or you have to learn how to read your own work as a critic.

Let us discuss the latter. We all have access to *me, myself, and I* as an editor.

Get away from what you have written for at least a day, but for longer if you have the time.

Next, print it out (if you can) and read it with a pen or pencil.

Circle or highlight text and make remarks in the left or right columns.

Write things like: *This is working; Do more; Expand;* or *This is not working,* or *Re-do.*

It is that simple. Don't complicate it.

Write more drafts as needed.

Make another pass.

And another. And another, as needed.

Is anything still missing? Mark that down, and pinpoint where.

Is anything still too long or not working? Mark that.

Rewrite as needed.

Make another pass to tighten everything.

Make a final pass to correct errors.

If you do this with everything you write, every time, you will learn how to edit.

And here is the best way to revise: *Write more slowly on your first draft.* Write, don't type. Or, type more slowly. Slow down. I purposely handwrite most everything, especially fiction, because it slows me down and looks messy enough to remind me that it is just a draft. Even when I type, I do so slowly and purposefully.

For a song or poem, after you write for thirty to sixty minutes, you should be about done. Sometimes it takes even less time than that.

When you write a short story, write for thirty to sixty minutes and then stop. Do the same thing the next day and the next, and keep going (likely for three to five days) until the story is finished. Then revise.

Do not write a story in one sitting unless it is meant to be a very short work.

By writing over the course of a week, the story develops; it is not rushed and does not lack detail. The story finds pace. It does not rush its ending. Most importantly, your brain spends that week working on it twenty-four hours a day, whether you're aware of it or not.

Keep everything you write . . . unless you have real need or desire to trash it.

Everything you write has the possibility of being recycled in a later work.

A final thought on writing and editing, and something I often say to my students, is: Learn to recognize where your bar is. By bar, I mean as in a high-jump. When you go through your work, note that line where you are working at your best. Not a show-off line, but one where you are, organically, working at your best. Understand that such a line, or perhaps a whole passage, is your (high jump) bar. Noting this forces you to *understand how good your work can be*, and that gives you a goal. The more you recognize these high levels, the more you will want to write and work toward them, and thus, the higher the bar will be set.

# A Parting Note

Writing is work, and it is important to know that. At the same time, if what you are doing is worthwhile, it will feel less like work and more like something you need in your life. If you follow the advice in this book, I believe you stand a good chance of finding worthwhile things to write about in a proven way.

Some small changes may exist between the published versions and the versions of my work herein. You can read many of my published stories and poems by entering "Richard Lee Zuras" into Google.

If you want to read even more of my work, my two novels, *The Bastard Year* and *The Honeymoon Corruption*, as well as my poetry collection, *Birds at the Post Office*, are available on Amazon.

If you want to listen to some of my song lyrics as actual songs, please visit Bandcamp and enter the name of my sons' band: "Holden & the Dangers" (where you will also find some lyrics not in this book). Even if you don't buy my sons' songs, kindly give them a listen.

# Why I Wrote This Book

I wrote this book because I have been fortunate. I studied under many esteemed writers and attended college and graduate school to study what I love to do. I spent my adult years teaching what I love and was afforded time and support to write by my university and my family.

It only makes sense to share my good fortune by being honest and open about my writing process. It only makes sense to share my experiences with others.

I also wrote this book because I believe my example is one rooted in the idea that hard work sometimes pays off. I am not naïve enough to believe anyone who works hard gets to do what they want as their career. I understand luck and circumstance.

Having said that, I do feel it was unlikely that someone like me could find such success. No one in my entire family lineage ever held a college degree until my brother and I earned ours. Neither of my parents ever took a single college class.

I started working at age eleven, delivering newspapers and mowing lawns. By seventeen, I had worked several jobs and began working full-time. I graduated middle of my high school class. My verbal SAT was not impressive. I struggled to pass my college courses in foreign language, astronomy, and calculus. I had not been a "star" student since middle school.

When I graduated college, it took me several years to be accepted into a creative writing graduate program. I worked retail and hotel jobs all through college and graduate school, which I attended piecemeal until I was accepted into my MFA program.

*I never stopped writing.*

My biggest talent is perseverance. My second talent is that I am highly teachable.

This book explores all the rest of my talent in detail. My talents are yours to utilize. My talents are accessible to you, because they are based in using memory and building fiction from truth.

I truly hope you succeed. If you find success, it will ultimately be your doing.

Cheers,

Rich

# *In Memory:*

## *Burnt Orange Chevrolet*

### (a song for my parents)

I see you've had your travels
Busted down and unraveled
Like my father's car he paid
An old burnt orange Chevrolet
That don't mean your stars can't shine
Your thirty-two now (that) ain't no crime
This life comes up short more or less
Lord knows that hands caress

Well you took my hand I took yours
I said darlin' what if we're sure
You're gone from him I'm gone from her
We can't go back to where we were
No we can't go back to where we were

I still own that burnt orange Chevy
It's in my past it's sittin' heavy
Busted down dead livin' out back
I could fix'er put'er on track

Darlin' what if I had it buried?
Darlin' what if we got married?
What if we just ran away?
Find honest work that pays?
Live our lives along the way
Like that burnt orange Chevrolet
It's funny how things work out
Maybe we should just drive south
Into an orange setting sun

Well you took my hand I took yours
I said darlin' what if we're sure
You're gone from him I'm gone from her
We can't go back to where we were
No we can't go back to where we were

We'll put the lights out make a run
Put the lights out darlin' make a run

## *Stories and Poems: Original Publications Stories*

"Runaway" in *Story Quarterly,* volume 41, pp. 432-44.
"Your Father and Mine" in *Chicago Quarterly Review*, Volume 7, pp. 15-24.
"Gestures" in *South Dakota Review* 40th Anniversary Issue, Volume 41, Numbers 1 & 2, pp. 64-76.
"Outside Beach" in *Weber Studies*, Volume 20, Number 2, pp. 94-104.
"The Wrestlers of Evangeline Parish" in *Big Muddy*, Volume 3, Issue 1, pp. 31-36.
"So Mother Left Father" in *Laurel Review*, Volume 26, Number 2, pp. 81-92.
"The Clipping of Maynard Jax" in *Passages North*, Volume 23, Number 1, pp. 29-34.
"1954" in *Xavier Review*, Volume 20, Number 2, pp. 100-103.

## *Poems*

"Three Rolls-Royces" in *The Pacific Review* 2019.
"Return of Lake Agassiz" in *Nourish* Inaugural Issue, 2018.
"Fontanel" in *Red Rock Review* Issue 17.
"House Hunting" in *Confrontation*, Volume 90/91, pp. 300-301.
"First Christmas without My Father" in *Milkwood Review (online).*
In addition, many of these poems can be found in *Birds at the Post Office,* Brandylane Publishers, Inc, 2020.

## *About the Author*

**Richard Lee Zuras** earned his MFA as a McNeese scholar under the auspices of Pulitzer Prize winner in fiction, Robert Olen Butler, and two-time Iowa Poetry Prize winner, John Wood. His stories and poems have appeared in dozens of literary journals including *Story Quarterly, South Dakota Review, Weber Journal, Big Muddy, Jabberwock Review, Lake Effect, Chicago Quarterly Review, Laurel Review, Yemassee, Xavier Review, Confrontation, Red Rock Review,* and *Passages North.* Richard has held writing conference scholarships at Bread Loaf, Wesleyan University, and Pirate's Alley Faulkner, and is the author of the novels *The Bastard Year*, and *The Honeymoon Corruption* as well as the poetry collection *Birds at the Post Office* (all Brandylane Publishers). Richard is a professor of English & creative writing at the University of Maine at Presque Isle where he has taught creative writing for more than twenty years. He lives with his wife, Kelly, two sons Everett and Holden, and a red Siberian husky named Indigo.

CPSIA information can be obtained
at www.ICGtesting.com
Printed in the USA
BVHW081147021222
653296BV00006B/142

9 781958 754030